Happy

27th Blessings

To You —

Nancy 2017

90 Devotions on Hymns from

OUR DAILY BREAD

Tune My Heart to Sing

DISCOVERY HOUSE

PUBLISHERS®

Discovery House Publishers is affiliated with RBC Ministries,
Grand Rapids, Michigan.

Requests for permission to quote from this book should be directed to:
Permissions Department, Discovery House Publishers,
P.O. Box 3566, Grand Rapids, MI 49501,
or contact us by e-mail at permissionsdept@dhp.org

Cover and interior design by Mark Veldheer

Cover and title page photograph © Exactostock/SuperStock

Interior photographs: page 4 © bns124/istock; page 9 © Anna Omelchenko/
istock; page 14 © Andrew Howe/istock; page 21 © AlpamayoPhoto/istock;
pages 27–28 © MarkVanDykePhotography/istock; page 32 © arinahabich/
istock; page 39 © mbogacz/istock; page 44 © MikeMcFarlane/istock;
pages 50–51 © HeikeKampe/istock; page 57 © kycstudio/istock; page 62
© Sara Winter/istock; pages 69, 121, and 125 © Mark Veldheer; pages 74–75
© Shelly Perry/istock; page 80 © Pgiam/istock; page 87 © Skabarcat/istock;
page 92 © franckreporter/istock; pages 98–99 © BernardBreton/istock;
page 105 © SteveByland/istock; page 110 © photosoul/istock; pages 116–117
© danielzgombic/istock; page 128 © malexeum/istock

ISBN: 978-1-62707-073-7

Printed in the United States of America

First printing in 2014

CONTENTS

FOREWORD

Years ago, while turning the dial of a shortwave radio one night in Kenya, I came across the voice of a man speaking rapidly in German until he pronounced the next singer's name: "Willie Nelson." I laughed aloud at the incongruity of being in East Africa and listening to a German disc jockey introduce an American country singer. How old-fashioned that seems in today's digital age. Yet, from the concert halls of great cities to the campfires of remote villages, "the universal language" of music still touches the hearts and souls of people across the globe.

How true this is among the followers of Jesus Christ. The story of God's work on earth began with music during creation when "the morning stars sang together, and all the sons of God [angels] shouted for joy" (Job 38:7). It continued with David's songs of adoration, confession, and thanksgiving, followed by Jeremiah's mournful lament over the spiritual failure of God's people. It will conclude when we sing His praise forever in heaven (Revelation 19:5). As we await that day, we are encouraged to "be filled with the Spirit, speaking to one another in psalms and hymns and spiritual songs, singing and making melody in your heart to the Lord" (Ephesians 5:18–19).

The songs of faith that mean most to us capture our deepest emotions and wrap them in words and melodies we remember. They guard us on the heights of success and guide us through the valleys of despair.

In 1757, 22-year-old Robert Robinson penned these words:

> *Come, Thou Fount of every blessing, tune my heart to sing Thy grace;*
> *Streams of mercy, never ceasing, call for songs of loudest praise.*
> *Teach me some melodious sonnet sung by flaming tongues above;*
> *Praise the mount—I'm fixed upon it—mount of Thy redeeming love.*

Tune My Heart to Sing celebrates the power of songs and hymns in our lives. What a privilege it is to pour out our pleas for help and our praise to our God of grace, whose love never fails!

—David McCasland

Thank God for Music

From God's Hymnal: 2 Chronicles 5:7–14

When the trumpeters and singers were as one, . . . the glory of the LORD filled the house of God. —2 CHRONICLES 5:13–14

Music plays a big part in the Bible. From Genesis to Revelation, God enlists musicians to work on His behalf. He uses music to call people to worship and to send them to war, to soothe ragged emotions and to ignite spiritual passion, to celebrate victories and to mourn losses. Music is an all-occasion, all-inclusive art form. There are followers and leaders, simple songs and complex songs, easy instruments and difficult instruments, melodies and harmonies, fast rhythms and slow rhythms, high notes and low notes.

Music is a wonderful metaphor for the church because everyone participates by doing what he or she does best. We all sing or play different notes at different times, but we all perform the same song. The better we know our parts, and the better we follow the conductor, the more beautiful the music.

One of the best uses for music is praise. When Solomon's temple was completed, the musicians praised and thanked God. As they did, "the glory of the LORD filled the house of God" (2 Chronicles 5:14).

We thank God for beautiful music, for it's like a preview of heaven, where the glory of God will dwell forever and where praise for Him will never cease.

—*Julie Ackerman Link*

Backstory

While musical styles can be controversial, we can also celebrate the fact that God can be glorified with the variety of music He has allowed to be developed. While some may prefer Fanny Crosby over Chris Tomlin (or vice versa), the beauty of unity in Christ is that we can overlook differences to stand together in praise of our heavenly Father in song.

♪ REFRAIN

"David spoke to the leaders of the Levites to appoint their brethren to be singers accompanied by instruments of music, stringed instruments, harps, and cymbals, by raising the voice with resounding joy." —1 Chronicles 15:16

Come Home

From God's Hymnal: Psalm 51:1–13

Restore to me the joy of Your salvation, and uphold me by Your generous Spirit.
—Psalm 51:12

As 19-year-old Amelia sat in the waiting room of her doctor's office, she recognized the familiar hymn "Softly and Tenderly Jesus Is Calling" playing over the speaker. It made her smile when she remembered the words. Perhaps a song with the lyrics "shadows are gathering, deathbeds are coming" was not the most appropriate background music for folks waiting to see the doctor!

Some find this old hymn too sentimental for their taste. But the message of the chorus can be encouraging for the wayward sinner:

> *Come home, come home;*
> *Ye who are weary, come home;*
> *Earnestly, tenderly, Jesus is calling—*
> *Calling, "O sinner, come home!"*

When a believer replaces God's will with his own, he will find himself in a backslidden condition, out of fellowship with God, and in an unenviable state. Although we sometimes yield to our self-centered nature, God is always ready to welcome us back. Because of His "lovingkindness" and "tender mercies," it gives Him joy when we forsake our rebellious ways, return to Him, and ask for forgiveness (Psalm 51:1–2; Luke 15).

Has your heart and mind slipped away from your Savior? Jesus is calling and waiting for you to come back home.

—*Cindy Hess Kasper*

REFRAIN

No matter how far you roam, you are just a short prayer from coming home.

Hidden in the Rock

From God's Hymnal: Psalm 18:30–36

The LORD is my rock, my fortress and my deliverer; my God is my rock, in whom I take refuge. —PSALM 18:2 (NIV)

The story is told of a young preacher named Augustus Toplady, who was taking a walk through the English countryside when a sudden storm swept across the landscape. Toplady spotted a wide rock formation with an opening—a cleft—where he sought shelter until the storm passed. As he sat out the deluge, he contemplated the connection between his shelter and God's help in life's storms.

He had no paper on which to write, but he found a playing card on the floor of the cavelike structure and began to write the words to the beloved hymn "Rock of Ages."

Written on that stormy day in 1775, this hymn has been a source of strength for Christians ever since.

> *Rock of ages, cleft for me,*
> *Let me hide myself in Thee;*
> *Let the water and the blood,*
> *From Thy wounded side which flowed,*
> *Be of sin the double cure,*
> *Save from wrath and make me pure.*

Backstory

The hymn "Rock of Ages" first appeared in the *Gospel Magazine* in 1775, which Augustus Toplady edited for two years. The magazine is still in publication.

Think of your struggles. Do you need a place to hide? Do you need someone to shelter you from life's assaults? Do you need the assurance that you've been forgiven? As Toplady experienced, we can find shelter and assurance in God.

Don't stand out in life's storms alone. Seek God's shelter. Ask Him to protect you. Make sure you have received His forgiveness. Get close to the Rock of Ages. It's life's safest spot.

—*Dave Branon*

 REFRAIN

No storm can overwhelm the believer safely surrounded by God's care.

By God's Help

From God's Hymnal: 1 Samuel 7:2–12

Then Samuel took a stone and set it up between Mizpah and Shen, and called its name Ebenezer, saying, "Thus far the LORD has helped us." —1 SAMUEL 7:12

The word *Ebenezer* in the hymn "Come, Thou Fount of Every Blessing" reminds us of a time when the people of Israel were trying to regain the close relationship they once had with God. Their spiritual leader, Samuel, told them that if they would abandon their foreign gods and return to the Lord wholeheartedly, He would deliver them from being oppressed by their enemy, the Philistines (1 Samuel 7:2–3).

When the people turned from their sin, God gave them victory. In response, "Samuel took a stone and set it up between Mizpah and Shen, and called its name Ebenezer, saying, 'Thus far the LORD has helped us' " (v. 12).

When we sing,

> Here I raise my Ebenezer—
> Hither by Thy help I've come;
> And I hope, by Thy good pleasure
> Safely to arrive at home

we are reminded that in our times of need we can always turn to God to find forgiveness and help. Whatever we have done, wherever we have wandered, He will receive and restore us by His grace.

A small stone on a desk or shelf can be our own Ebenezer—a powerful, visible reminder that by God's help we have come this far in life, and He will see us through to the end.

—*David McCasland*

REFRAIN

A stone of remembrance worked for Samuel. What reminds you of God's help?

The Good Story

But they found the stone rolled away from the tomb. Then they went in and did not find the body of the Lord Jesus. —LUKE 24:2–3

People tend to remember negative images more than they do positive ones, according to an experiment conducted at the University of Chicago. While people claim that they want to turn away from the barrage of bad news in the media—reports on tragedies, diseases, economic downturns—this study suggests that their minds are drawn to the stories.

Katherine Hankey (1834–1911) was more interested in the "good news." She had a great desire to see young women come to know Christ. In 1866, she became very ill. As she lay in bed, she thought about all those with whom she had shared the story of Jesus' redemption, and she wished that someone would visit and comfort her with "the old, old story." That's when she wrote a poem that later became the hymn "Tell Me the Old, Old Story."

> *Tell me the story slowly, that I may take it in—*
> *That wonderful redemption, God's remedy for sin.*
> *Tell me the story often, for I forget so soon;*
> *The early dew of morning has passed away at noon.*

We never tire of hearing the story that because of His great love God sent His one and only Son to this earth (John 3:16). Jesus lived a perfect life, took our sin upon himself when He was crucified, and three days later rose again (Luke 23:44–24:3). When we receive Him as our Savior, we are given eternal life and become His children (John 1:12).

Tell someone the old, old story of Jesus and His love. That person just might need some good news.

—*Anne Cetas*

Backstory

According to Ira Sankey in his book *My Life and the Story of the Gospel Hymns*, Katherine Hankey's poem was read at a YMCA convention in 1867. William Howard Doane heard the poem and later wrote the music for it while traveling on a stagecoach. Doane wrote the music for several Fanny Crosby songs as well.

 REFRAIN

The gospel story may be *old*, but it is definitely still good *news*.

Is It Well?

From God's Hymnal: Philippians 4:4–7

The peace of God, which surpasses all understanding, will guard your hearts and minds through Christ Jesus. —Philippians 4:7

As the high school chorale prepared to sing Horatio G. Spafford's classic hymn, "It Is Well with My Soul," a teen stepped forward to tell the song's familiar history. Spafford wrote the song while on a ship that was near the spot at sea where his four daughters perished in a collision of two ocean-going vessels.

As I listened to that introduction and then the words sung by the teenagers, a flood of emotions washed over me. "Where his four daughters perished" were hard words to grasp as I listened again to Spafford's words of faith. Having lost one teenage daughter suddenly myself, I find the idea of losing four unfathomable.

How could it be "well" for Spafford in his grief? I hear the words "When peace, like a river, attendeth my way" and remember where peace can be found. Paul says in Philippians 4 that it can be found as our heart-prayers are voiced to God (v. 6). By trustful praying, we unburden our hearts, divest our anxieties, and release the grip on our grief. And we can gain "the peace of God" (v. 7)—an inexplicable, divine calmness of spirit. This peace supersedes our ability to understand our circumstances (v. 7), and it is a guard on our heart, through Jesus, that protects us enough to allow us to whisper, even in the pain, "It is well with my soul."

—Dave Branon

Backstory

Horatio and Anna Spafford lost their only son to pneumonia in 1870 before losing their daughters (Annie, 11; Margaret, 9; Bessie, 5; and Tanetta, 2) in the November 22, 1873, shipwreck of the *Ville du Havre* while Anna and the girls were on their way to a vacation in England.

 REFRAIN

God can take what isn't good in our eyes and make it into something that is well in His.

The Fairest

From God's Hymnal: Revelation 5:8–14

"Worthy is the Lamb who was slain!" — REVELATION 5:12

When I first became a Christian and started attending church at age nineteen, I immediately fell in love with the great hymns of the faith. My heart overflowed with joy and thanksgiving as we sang of God's love for us in Christ. Soon one of my favorite hymns (written in the late 1600s) became "Fairest Lord Jesus!" I love the simplicity of the melody and the awesomeness of the One exalted in these words:

Fair is the sunshine,
Fairer still the moonlight,
And all the twinkling starry host: Jesus shines brighter,
Jesus shines purer than all the angels heaven can boast.
Beautiful Savior!
Lord of the nations!
Son of God and Son of Man!
Glory and honor, praise, adoration
Now and forevermore be Thine!

Backstory

Not much is known about the history of "Fairest Lord Jesus." It appears to have been published in English for the first time in 1677. The melody is from Silesia, a land between Poland and the Czech Republic.

God's Son, whom we sing about in this song, came to this earth, lived a perfect life, and gave himself for us on the cross (Luke 23:33). He arose from the grave (Luke 24:6) and is now seated at God's right hand (Hebrews 1:3). One day we'll join in worship with thousands upon thousands and say: "Blessing and honor and glory and power be to Him who sits on the throne, and to the Lamb, forever and ever!" (Revelation 5:13). Maybe we'll sing "Fairest Lord Jesus!" too.

Until then, let's allow Jesus to be "the fairest" above all in our personal lives by seeking wisdom from His Word and following in His ways.

—*Anne Cetas*

♪ REFRAIN

As we live and interact with others, let's try to make "Jesus shine brighter."

He Watches Me

From God's Hymnal: Matthew 10:16–31

Do not fear therefore; you are of more value than many sparrows.
—MATTHEW 10:31

One Sunday morning at church, we sang "His Eye Is on the Sparrow" as a congregational hymn. It was a rare opportunity to give voice to a song usually performed by a soloist.

During the first chorus, I noticed a friend who was weeping so hard he couldn't sing. Knowing a bit of what he had been through recently, I recognized his tears as ones of joy at realizing that, no matter what our situation, God sees, knows, and cares for us.

Jesus said, "Are not two sparrows sold for a copper coin? And not one of them falls to the ground apart from your Father's will. But the very hairs of your head are all numbered. Do not fear therefore; you are of more value than many sparrows" (Matthew 10:29–31). The Lord spoke these words to His twelve disciples as He sent them out to teach, heal, and bear witness of Him to "the lost sheep of the house of Israel" (v. 6). He told them that even though they would face persecution for His sake, they should not be afraid, even of death (vv. 22–26).

When threatening circumstances press us to lose hope, we can find encouragement in the words of this song: "I sing because I'm happy, I sing because I'm free. For His eye is on the sparrow, and I know He watches me." We are under His watchful care.

—*David McCasland*

Backstory

The writer of the words to "His Eye Is on the Sparrow," Civilla Martin, said she heard a disabled friend answer a question about the secret to her happiness despite her troubles by saying, "His eye is on the sparrow, and I know He's watching me." Singer Ethel Waters used the song title as the title of her autobiography.

♪ REFRAIN

If you have ever watched with fascination and admiration the work of a little sparrow, you have a glimpse of the joy God has in watching each of us.

Something to Sing About

From God's Hymnal: Psalm 147

Praise the LORD! For it is good to sing praises to our God. —PSALM 147:1

I understand why I was never asked to join a choir or sing a solo. Musical talent was never one of my gifts. I discovered this at nine years of age when I was outside on our farm one day singing lustily. My mother opened the door and asked, "Is one of the calves sick? I think I just heard one."

My mother's words have never kept me from praising God in song, however. And when I preached somewhere, I enthusiastically joined in congregational singing (making sure, of course, not to stand too close to the microphone).

God's great salvation fills me with gratitude, and one way to express my joy is to sing about it. That's why I'm puzzled by people who say they are Christians but admit that they seldom attend church services, almost never listen to Christian music, and find singing hymns and listening to sermons boring. I can understand nonbelievers saying this because they know neither God nor the joy of salvation. But believers do!

Reflect often and deeply on the riches you have in Christ. If you feel joyful, you will want to praise the Lord. And even if you are a poor singer like me, you'll still say a hearty "Amen" to the psalmist's words: "It is good to sing praises to our God" (Psalm 147:1).

—*Herb Vander Lugt*

 REFRAIN

Worship is made up of many components—and one we would do well not to neglect is music and the shared musical expression of love for God in the church.

The Value of "Hums"

From God's Hymnal: Psalm 126:1–3

Speaking to one another in psalms and hymns and spiritual songs.
—Ephesians 5:19

Do you know why bees hum? It's because they can't remember the words!

Ironically, that old joke reminds me of a serious story I read about a man awaiting heart bypass surgery. He was aware that people die during surgery. As he thought about all that could go wrong, he felt very much alone.

Then an orderly walked into his room to take him to surgery. As the young man began to push the patient's gurney along the corridor, the patient heard the orderly humming the ancient Irish hymn "Be Thou My Vision." It prompted his memories of lush green fields and the ancient stone ruins of Ireland, the land of his birth. The hymn flooded his soul like a fresh breath of home. When the orderly finished with that song, he hummed Horatio Spafford's hymn, "It Is Well with My Soul."

When they stopped outside the surgical suite, the patient thanked the orderly for the hymns. "God has used you this day," he said, "to remove my fears and restore my soul." "How so?" the orderly asked in surprise. "Your 'hums' brought God to me," the man replied.

"The LORD has done great things for us" (Psalm 126:3). He has filled our heart with song. He may even use our "hums" to restore someone's soul.

—*David Roper*

Backstory

"Be Thou My Vision" originated more than 1,000 years ago in Ireland. It was translated into English by Mary Byrne and popularized in the early twentieth century.

🎵 REFRAIN

The beauty of God-honoring music is that even the tunes by themselves can pour hope into our souls when we need it the most.

Invisible Man

From God's Hymnal: John 14:5–20

Looking unto Jesus, the author and finisher of our faith, who for the joy that was set before Him endured the cross. —HEBREWS 12:2

As a boy, I was fascinated by the book *The Invisible Man*. The main character played an elaborate game of hide-and-seek, staying just out of reach of mere mortals "cursed" with a visible nature. To have a physical presence, he wore clothes and wrapped his face in bandages. When it was time to escape, he simply removed everything and disappeared.

I wonder if we have similar thoughts about our unseen God. We feel He's beyond our reach, as expressed in a stanza of one of my favorite hymns:

> *Immortal, invisible, God only wise,*
> *In light inaccessible*
> *Hid from our eyes.*

Backstory

Walter Chalmers Smith, who had two doctoral degrees, wrote "Immortal, Invisible" while pastoring a church in Scotland in 1867. He based the song on 1 Timothy 1:17.

Yet, while declaring the wonder of God, the hymn speaks of a God who is not just invisible:

> *All praise we would render—O help us to see*
> *'Tis only the splendor of light hideth Thee!*

We perceive that God is distant, far off, inaccessible, and hidden. But we need a God who is accessible, and we wonder how to have a meaningful relationship with Him. We will never fully comprehend what God is like. Yet He himself is accessible to us. In part, that is why Jesus came—to "show us the Father" (John 14:8) and to bring us close to Him, because "He is the image of the invisible God, the firstborn over all creation" (Colossians 1:15).

Our God is invisible—beyond our limited comprehension. Thankfully, though, Jesus came to show us how near He really is.

—*Bill Crowder*

♪ REFRAIN

Our inability to see God should never stop us from seeing how much He loves us and what He has done for us.

Thanksgiving All Year

From God's Hymnal: 1 Chronicles 16:8–13, 23–36

Oh, give thanks to the LORD, for He is good! —1 CHRONICLES 16:34

The beautiful hymn, "We Plow the Fields," is often sung in the United States during the Thanksgiving holiday period in November. For me, it conjures images of families sharing a traditional feast during the harvest season.

But I was surprised when I heard it sung in church during the month of June, far removed from its traditional holiday context. It reminded me that giving thanks to God for His goodness and provision is to be a continuing celebration for His people.

For a special occasion of national celebration, King David wrote a song to guide his people in praising God on that day: "Oh, give thanks to the LORD! Call upon His name; make known His deeds among the peoples! . . . Let the hearts of those rejoice who seek the LORD!" (1 Chronicles 16:8, 10). But the song endured as part of Israel's songbook of ongoing praise (Psalm 105:1–15).

Two centuries ago, Matthias Claudius wrote:

> *We thank Thee, then, O Father, for all things bright and good,*
> *The seedtime and the harvest, our life, our health, our food:*
> *No gifts have we to offer for all Thy love imparts,*
> *But that which Thou desirest, our humble, thankful hearts.*
> *All good gifts around us are sent from heaven above;*
> *Then thank the Lord, O thank the Lord for all His love.*

We have so much to be thankful for every day. God continually provides for all our needs. So let's make Thanksgiving a yearlong celebration.

—*David McCasland*

Backstory

Matthias Claudius, the son of a pastor, was a German poet and editor who died in Hamburg in 1815. He sometimes used the pen name "Asmus."

REFRAIN

Any day that ends with the letter "y" is a good day for thanksgiving.

Harvest Home

From God's Hymnal: James 4:13–17; 5:7–11

You also be patient. Establish your hearts, for the coming of the Lord is at hand.
—JAMES 5:8

The hymn "Come, Ye Thankful People, Come" is often sung at Christian services of thanksgiving. Written in 1844 by Henry Alford, it begins with thanks to God for crops safely gathered in before winter. But it is more than gratefulness for the bounty of the land. The hymn ends by focusing on God's "harvest" of His people when Christ returns:

> *Even so, Lord, quickly come*
> *To Thy final harvest-home:*
> *Gather Thou Thy people in,*
> *Free from sorrow, free from sin;*
> *There, forever purified,*
> *In Thy presence to abide:*
> *Come, with all Thine angels, come—*
> *Raise the glorious harvest-home.*

As we give thanks for material needs supplied, it's essential to remember that our plans are uncertain and our lives are a vapor that quickly disappears (James 4:14). James encourages us to be like a farmer waiting for his crops to grow and mature. "You also be patient. Establish your hearts, for the coming of the Lord is at hand" (5:8).

As we thank God for His faithful provision for our needs, let's turn our thoughts to the promised return of Jesus Christ. In patient expectation, we live for Him and look for the day when He will come to gather His glorious harvest home.

—David McCasland

REFRAIN

It's possible to continue God's work on earth while watching for His return.

What Child Is This?

From God's Hymnal: Luke 2:25–35

This Child is destined for the fall and rising of many in Israel, . . . that the thoughts of many hearts may be revealed. —Luke 2:34–35

One of our most beloved Christmas carols was written in 1865 by William Dix, an Englishman who managed a maritime insurance company and loved to write hymns. Fashioned after the English melody "Greensleeves," the song is not always sung the same way. Some versions use the latter half of the first verse as a chorus for the other verses:

> *This, this is Christ the King, Whom shepherds guard*
> *   and angels sing:*
> *Haste, haste, to bring Him laud—*
> *The Babe, the Son of Mary.*

But in other versions, each stanza is unique. The second verse, rarely sung today, looks beyond the manger to the cross:

> *Why lies He in such mean estate where ox and ass are*
> *   feeding?*
> *Good Christian, fear—for sinners here the silent*
> *   Word is pleading.*
> *Nails, spear shall pierce Him through, the cross be*
> *   borne for me, for you.*
> *Hail, hail the Word made flesh, the Babe, the Son of*
> *   Mary.*

Simeon said to Mary, "This Child is destined for the fall and rising of many in Israel, and for a sign which will be spoken against (yes, a sword will pierce through your own soul also), that the thoughts of many hearts may be revealed" (Luke 2:34–35).

The Child of Christmas came to be our Savior. "Joy, joy for Christ is born, the Babe, the Son of Mary."

—*David McCasland*

Backstory

This song has been recorded over the years by such stars as Johnny Mathis, the Lettermen, Tony Bennett, Andy Williams, MercyMe, Kevin Max, and Josh Groban.

⚮ REFRAIN

Never before nor ever since has such a Baby been born!

Source of Gladness

From God's Hymnal: 2 Corinthians 6:3–12

As sorrowful, yet always rejoicing; as poor, yet making many rich; as having nothing, and yet possessing all things. —2 CORINTHIANS 6:10

Paul Gerhardt, a pastor in Germany during the seventeenth century, had every reason not to be glad. His wife and four of his children died; the Thirty Years' War brought death and devastation across Germany; church conflict and political interference filled his life with distress. Yet despite great personal suffering, he wrote more than 130 hymns, many of them characterized by joy and devotion to Jesus Christ.

One of Gerhardt's hymns, "Holy Spirit, Source of Gladness," contains this verse:

> *Let that love which knows no measure*
> *Now in quickening showers descend,*
> *Bringing us the richest treasures*
> *Man can wish or God can send;*
> *Hear our earnest supplication,*
> *Every struggling heart release;*
> *Rest upon this congregation,*
> *Spirit of untroubled peace.*

Backstory

In addition to "Holy Spirit," Paul Gerhardt also wrote the famous "O Sacred Head, Now Wounded" based on a Latin poem of the Middle Ages.

Because God's abounding love is poured into our hearts by the Holy Spirit (Romans 5:5), is there any situation in which we cannot experience the joy He gives?

During a time of great personal hardship, Paul described his experience as being "sorrowful, yet always rejoicing; as poor, yet making many rich; as having nothing, and yet possessing all things" (2 Corinthians 6:10).

Pain and sorrow are inescapable facts of life. Yet the Holy Spirit is our source of gladness, "bringing us the richest treasures man can wish or God can send."

—*David McCasland*

REFRAIN

There is no joy in suffering, but we can find joy if we trust Christ in such times.

Everlasting Arms

From God's Hymnal: Deuteronomy 33:26–29

The eternal God is your refuge, and underneath are the everlasting arms.
—DEUTERONOMY 33:27

After a pre-concert rehearsal in New York City's Carnegie Hall, Randall Atcheson sat on stage alone. He had successfully navigated the intricate piano compositions of Beethoven, Chopin, and Liszt for the evening program, and with only minutes remaining before the doors opened, he wanted to play one more piece for himself. What came from his heart and his hands was an old hymn by Elisha Hoffman:

> *What have I to dread,*
> *What have I to fear,*
> *Leaning on the everlasting arms?*
> *I have blessed peace*
> *With my Lord so near,*
> *Leaning on the everlasting arms.*

Those words echo the truth in the final blessing of Moses: "There is no one like the God of Jeshurun, who rides the heavens to help you, and in His excellency on the clouds. The eternal God is your refuge, and underneath are the everlasting arms" (Deuteronomy 33:26–27).

What a gift we have in our own arms and hands—they can swing a hammer, hold a child, or help a friend. But while our strength is limited, God's boundless power on our behalf is expressed in might and gentle care. "Behold, the LORD's hand is not shortened, that it cannot save" (Isaiah 59:1). "He will gather the lambs with His arm, and carry them in His bosom" (Isaiah 40:11).

Whatever challenge or opportunity we face, there is security and peace in God's everlasting arms.

—*David McCasland*

Backstory

Prolific songwriter Elisha Hoffman (1839–1929) wrote more than 2,000 published songs while pastoring churches in Ohio, Michigan, and Illinois. Others include "Down at the Cross," "Have Thine Own Way, Lord," and "Are You Washed in the Blood?"

REFRAIN

No strength is greater than the power of God's mighty arms.

Let It Shine

From God's Hymnal: Matthew 5:1–16

Let your light so shine before men, that they may see your good works and glorify your Father in heaven. —MATTHEW 5:16

As a young boy, I enjoyed singing hymns in church like "Throw Out the Lifeline" and "Let the Lower Lights Be Burning," which used images of shipwreck and danger at sea to illustrate our spiritual responsibility to others. However, living in landlocked Oklahoma I had never seen the ocean, and my nautical experience was limited to sailing Matchbox® boats on mud puddles. I knew the words but had little concept of how to rescue a "fainting, struggling seaman."

But in Sunday school, when we sang "This little light of mine, I'm gonna let it shine," it seemed perfectly clear what I should do. Jesus said, "You are the light of the world. . . . Let your light so shine before men, that they may see your good works and glorify your Father in heaven" (Matthew 5:14, 16). We memorized the Beatitudes (vv. 3–12) as an example of how we could let our lives shine for Him.

As a child I understood that I should not be ashamed to live for Jesus. A secret Christian was like a lamp hidden under a basket instead of shining openly where it could help others (v. 15).

Today, people around us are in spiritual danger and darkness. Young or old, we can let our light shine for Him and for them.

—*David McCasland*

REFRAIN

How can our little light make a difference? By using it to point others to the Great Light: Jesus Christ our Lord.

Worship

From God's Hymnal: Psalm 150

Let everything that has breath praise the LORD. Praise the LORD! —PSALM 150:6

Church people can get quite upset about music. Some Christians feel that God is particularly drawn to old hymns sung to the strains of a pipe organ. Others are sure that God enjoys choruses sung over and over again. Some clap their hands when they sing while others fold their arms. Many modern Christians would be quite unsettled if they had to worship with the ancient Israelites. They might resent the loud, boisterous music. And talk about a praise band! The instruments in the orchestra—wind, string, and percussion together—sounded out their hymns to God. In the middle of the worship, people danced. Large choirs sang their anthems heralding God's greatness. Unfortunately, many Christians would hear only the noise. What is worse, they would be angry because they couldn't fire the worship leader or quit and join another church.

One thing we dare not overlook in our disagreements about worship: God demands our praise! That is not negotiable. There is nothing or no one in the universe more worthy of praise than our Lord himself.

Don't waste your breath arguing about how to worship. Just worship! "Let everything that has breath praise the LORD. Praise the LORD!" (Psalm 150:6).

—*Haddon Robinson*

REFRAIN

As we sing praises to our Lord, let us remember that our task is to concentrate on God and to direct our thoughts, hopes, and admiration toward Him.

He Lives!

From God's Hymnal: Acts 1:1–10

He also presented Himself alive after His suffering by many infallible proofs.
—Acts 1:3

When the World Trade Center towers came crashing to the ground in a deafening roar of billowing debris, citizens of New York experienced what many people in other parts of the world had already known—the fear of terrorism. Subsequent attacks in other countries have heightened the concern that mankind may be spiraling toward self-destruction.

All the unrest in the world might make us think that our future is very bleak. We might even conclude that this is not the kind of world in which to raise children.

Yet one shining hope remains that can brighten our view of the future. Bill Gaither captured it in his song titled "Because He Lives." The idea for this song came to him in the late 1960s, a time of social unrest in the US and conflict in Southeast Asia. His wife Gloria was expecting a child, and they felt that it was a poor time to bring a child into the world. But when their son was born, Bill thought of the living Savior and decided his child would be okay because our Savior lives.

Two thousand years ago Jesus rose from the grave and gave "many infallible proofs" that He was alive (Acts 1:3). That's why we can keep going in the face of fear. Because Jesus lives, we can face tomorrow.

—*Dave Branon*

Backstory

Before Bill and Gloria Gaither became known worldwide for their uplifting gospel songs and their warm, inviting, down-home style of presentation, they were both schoolteachers. Bill taught English for eight years before he and Gloria (who taught French) went into music full-time.

 Refrain

The life Jesus gives us through His life and death provides purpose and hope in the midst of discouraging circumstances.

When Jesus Comes In

From God's Hymnal: Mark 5:1–20

Daughter, your faith has made you well. Go in peace, and be healed of your affliction. —Mark 5:34

In 1932, as the United States was undergoing a financial breakdown, missionary Robert Cummings was suffering an emotional breakdown. As he carried on his evangelistic ministry with his wife in India, he became obsessed by blasphemous and sinful thoughts so overwhelming that he felt cast aside by God and eternally lost. Hospital care and therapy were of no help. His wife brought him back to the US where he was placed in a private mental facility.

For two more years Robert underwent indescribable emotional agony. Then one morning he knelt beside his bed begging for relief. God answered dramatically with the words of a poem by James Procter:

> *My soul is night, my heart is steel—*
> *I cannot see, I cannot feel;*
> *For light, for life, I must appeal*
> *In simple faith to Jesus.*

As Robert repeated those lines, peace surged through his soul. Dread vanished from his heart and he was filled with joy and gratitude. Then a hymn by William Sleeper welled up from the depths of his memory, which he sang with one significant change. For him it wasn't, "Jesus, I come to Thee," but "Jesus has come to me."

—*Vernon Grounds*

Backstory

William Sleeper's commission in life was to start churches. He planted three churches in Maine and one in Massachusetts. Eventually, he met a song leader named George Stebbins. The two collaborated on the song "Ye Must Be Born Again."

♪ REFRAIN

The pathway to Jesus is marked by times of searching and times of receiving. We need to continually seek Him—knowing that He touches us where we are.

Our Message

From God's Hymnal: 1 Corinthians 2:1–8

I determined not to know anything among you except Jesus Christ and Him crucified. —1 CORINTHIANS 2:2

I've heard people say that the Lord sometimes uses simple hymns to impress them with profound truths. Songs like "He Lives," "Great Is Thy Faithfulness," or "Jesus Saves" have jolted them as if they were hearing these truths for the first time.

Something similar happened to me in 1986. I attended a convention that drew 10,000 evangelists from many countries. Our unified concern was to bring God's plan of salvation to our lost and needy world. As I went to seminars and listened to brilliant speakers, I began to wonder if the urgent task of evangelism was beyond me. Then a singer was invited to the platform. My spirit soared with reassurance and confidence as her rich voice proclaimed, "People need the Lord!" She reminded us in song that people all around us need to hear about Jesus and put their faith in Him.

Sharing the gospel means sharing Christ, His death, and His resurrection with people lost in sin. Paul said he didn't minister with eloquence or worldly wisdom. He chose to know nothing "except Jesus Christ and Him crucified" (1 Corinthians 2:2).

Yes, there is much knowledge to be learned, but the key to that knowledge is to know the Lord. That's why people need Him. Remember, our message is Christ.

—*Joanie Yoder*

Backstory

Although Steve Green made "People Need the Lord" famous, it was written by Greg Nelson and Phill McHugh. They came up with the idea while eating at a restaurant and noticing the empty look in the eyes of their waitress. "She needs the Lord," one of them remarked, and the idea was born.

REFRAIN

In a consumer-driven society, it's hard to get people to see beyond their wants to their greatest need: salvation through Christ.

Joy to the World

From God's Hymnal: Psalm 98

The LORD has made known His salvation; His righteousness He has revealed in the sight of the nations. —PSALM 98:2

While walking home from a church service in Southampton, England, twenty-year-old Isaac Watts told his father that the metrical psalms sung at their services lacked the dignity and beauty that should characterize hymns used in worship. His father encouraged him to try to create something better. So in the year 1694, Isaac Watts began writing hymns and eventually put the book of Psalms into rhyming meter for worship.

Watts took the prophetic references to the coming Messiah in the Psalms and expressed them in their New Testament fulfillment. His hymns proclaimed that Jesus Christ is Savior and Lord. When Watts came to Psalm 98, he wrote:

> *Joy to the world! The Lord is come!*
> *Let earth receive her King;*
> *Let every heart prepare Him room,*
> *And heaven and nature sing.*
> *Joy to the earth! The Savior reigns!*
> *Let men their songs employ;*
> *While fields and floods, rocks, hills, and plains*
> *Repeat the sounding joy.*

This hymn has become a favorite of the Christmas season. It calls us to acknowledge Christ as Savior and King and to open our hearts to His rule of love and grace.

The psalmist wrote, "Oh, sing to the LORD a new song!" (98:1). Isaac Watts did just that in his proclamation that Christ has come, and we can rejoice in Him.

—*David McCasland*

Backstory

Isaac Watts felt the psalms "ought to be translated in such a manner as we have reason to believe David would have composed them if he had lived in our day." This Watts attempted to do in his hymns, combining ideas expressed in the psalms with frequent references to the cross of Christ.

REFRAIN

What better proclamation to share with a troubled world than these eight words: "Joy to the world; the Lord is come!"

Friendship with Jesus

From God's Hymnal: John 15:9–17

You are My friends if you do whatever I command you. —JOHN 15:14

Joseph Scriven (1819–1886), writer of the much-loved hymn "What a Friend We Have in Jesus," knew the pain of heartache and loneliness. His bride-to-be drowned the evening before their wedding. Later a second fiancée died of pneumonia, and again his hopes for marriage were dashed. Yet Christ's friendship sustained him.

Backstory

Born in Ireland, Joseph Scriven moved to Canada, where he led a life of restraint and poverty—given to share all he had with people in need.

Anyone can have that same comforting friendship. At one point in my life, I came to know John, a recovering addict who at the lowest point in his life put his faith in Jesus. He sensed that the Lord was asking him, "Do you want a friend forever?" As John wept over his broken condition, he sobbed, "Yes," and Christ came into his life.

Later, John told me that he urgently needed a liver transplant. "You know, John," I said, "cynical people might say, 'Some friend Jesus has turned out to be, considering your condition.'" John replied, "But I'm not saying that." Then he added, "I certainly don't want to leave my family. But however it goes, Jesus remains my friend."

In John 15:14, Jesus said that we are His friends, suggesting that this is a two-way relationship. But He added one important condition: We must walk obediently with Him. Only then can we testify, "Whatever happens, Jesus remains my friend."

—*Joanie Yoder*

REFRAIN

There is no friend like the One who died for you and has the ability to be your forever friend. That Friend is Jesus.

The Wondrous Cross

[Jesus], bearing His cross, went out to a place called the Place of the Skull, which is called in Hebrew, Golgotha, where they crucified Him. —JOHN 19:17–18

Mahatma Gandhi asked some missionaries who visited him during one of his numerous fasts to sing a hymn for him. "Which hymn?" they asked. "The one that expresses all that is deepest in your faith," he replied. They thought for a moment and then with full hearts sang these words written by Isaac Watts:

> *When I survey the wondrous cross*
> *On which the Prince of glory died,*
> *My richest gain I count but loss,*
> *And pour contempt on all my pride.*

Yes, there is something wondrous about the cross that stirs our hearts. When we think back to Calvary, our souls are saddened and yet thrilled with the wonder of it all. With heartfelt gratitude we exclaim, "Thank you, Lord, for saving my soul!"

When George Briggs was governor of Massachusetts in the mid-1800s, three of his friends visited the Holy Land. While they were there, they climbed Golgotha's slope and cut from the hilltop a stick to be used as a cane. On their return they presented it to the governor, saying, "We want you to know that when we stood on Calvary, we thought of you." He accepted the gift with gratitude and then remarked, "I appreciate your consideration of me, gentlemen, but I am still more thankful for Another who thought of me there!"

Yes, Jesus thought of you and me when hanging there in agony. A life of gratitude would be our appropriate response.

—*Henry Bosch*

Backstory

At the time Isaac Watts wrote "When I Survey the Wondrous Cross" in 1707, the tradition was for the church to sing songs with lyrics taken exclusively from Scripture— especially the Old Testament. This song departed from that pattern, yet it was well accepted.

♪ REFRAIN

The cross carried not only the weight of Jesus' body and the burden of our sins but also our highest hopes for redemption.

A Unique Choir

From God's Hymnal: Romans 15:5–13

That you may with one mind and one mouth glorify the God and Father of our Lord Jesus Christ. —ROMANS 15:6

When Mitch Miller died in July 2010, most people remembered him as the man who invited everyone to sing along. On his popular 1960s TV program *Sing Along with Mitch*, an all-male chorus sang well-loved songs while the words appeared on the screen so viewers could join in. A *Los Angeles Times* obituary cited Miller's belief that one reason for the program's success was the appeal of his chorus: "I always made a point of hiring singers who were tall, short, bald, round, fat, whatever—everyday-looking guys." From that unified diversity came beautiful music in which everyone was invited to participate.

In Romans 15, Paul called for unity among the followers of Christ—"that you may with one mind and one mouth glorify the God and Father of our Lord Jesus Christ" (v. 6). From several Old Testament passages, he spoke of Gentiles and Jews together singing praise to God (vv. 9–12). A unity that had been considered impossible became reality as people who had been deeply divided began thanking God together for His mercy shown in Christ. Like them, we are filled with joy, peace, and hope "by the power of the Holy Spirit" (v. 13).

What a unique "choir" we belong to, and what a privilege it is to sing along!

—*David McCasland*

Backstory

Each congregation comprises its own unique choir—allowing singers and non-singers alike the anonymity of singing praises together to God. In the Bible, perhaps one of the first choirs was the children of Israel as they sang the Song of Moses found in Exodus 15:1–18.

REFRAIN

The glory of congregational singing is the mixture of generations and socio-economic groups into one choir voicing a unified message of God's love and salvation.

God Reigns

From God's Hymnal: Psalm 46

The LORD reigns; let the earth rejoice. —PSALM 97:1

In Germany in the late 1930s, young Dr. Herbert Gezork was fortunate that he was sentenced to exile instead of execution. Yet the night before his departure for America, he wandered the streets of Hamburg in deep despair. He kept asking, "What hope is there in a world where demonic forces are triumphing?"

Then Gezork heard music coming from a church. He walked in and listened as the organist played Martin Luther's hymn "A Mighty Fortress Is Our God." The words of one stanza came to mind:

> *And though this world, with devils filled, should*
> > *threaten to undo us,*
> *We will not fear, for God hath willed His truth to*
> > *triumph through us.*

Gradually the truth of the lyrics sank into Dr. Gerzork's soul and brought him peace.

The words of Psalm 46 can do the same for us in times of despair. The psalmist declares God's mastery over the forces of nature (vv. 1–3) and His triumph over the nations (vv. 4–10). The LORD will judge the wicked and rescue His people. To the restless and rebellious He says, "Be still, and know that I am God; . . . I will be exalted in the earth!" (v. 10). We who know Him can joyfully exclaim, "The LORD of hosts is with us; the God of Jacob is our refuge" (v. 11). Our God reigns!

—*Herb Vander Lugt*

Backstory

Written in his native German by Martin Luther in the late 1520s, "A Mighty Fortress Is Our God" was first translated into English in 1539 by Myles Coverdale, a noted Bible translator. The translation we sing today was penned in 1853 by Frederick Hedge.

REFRAIN

There is no better refuge in this world than the One who created it and provided a plan of salvation for every person He created.

Time to Praise

From God's Hymnal: Psalm 30

You have turned for me my mourning into dancing. —PSALM 30:11

It was the worst of times. In the first half of the seventeenth century, Germany was in the midst of wars and famine and pestilence. In the city of Eilenburg lived a pastor by the name of Martin Rinkart (1586–1649).

During one especially oppressive period, Rinkart conducted up to fifty funerals a day as a plague swept through the town and as the Thirty Years' War wreaked its own terror on the people. Among those whom Rinkart buried were members of his own family.

Yet during those years of darkness and despair, when death and destruction greeted each new day, Pastor Rinkart wrote sixty-six sacred songs and hymns. Among them was the song "Now Thank We All Our God." As sorrow crouched all around him, Rinkart wrote:

> *Now thank we all our God*
> *With hearts and hands and voices,*
> *Who wondrous things hath done,*
> *In whom His world rejoices;*
> *Who from our mothers' arms*
> *Hath blessed us on our way*
> *With countless gifts of love,*
> *And still is ours today.*

Rinkart demonstrated a valuable lesson for us all: Thankfulness does not have to wait for prosperity and peace. It's always a good time to praise God for the "wondrous things" He has done.

—Dave Branon

Backstory

In addition to the plague, Eilenburg also suffered through a severe famine and even monetary abuse from high government taxes. Yet Martin Rinkart gave of everything he had to help his people and to remind them to be grateful.

REFRAIN

What time is it? It's time to give praise and honor to our Almighty God.

Worthy of Praise

From God's Hymnal: Psalm 150

Praise Him according to His excellent greatness! —Psalm 150:2

A well-known theologian was asked to explain the gospel. In response, he simply quoted from a children's hymn, "Jesus loves me! This I know, for the Bible tells me so."

The great truths of our faith can be expressed in very simple terms, such as "God is love" or "Christ died for our sins and rose again." They can also be expressed in profound doctrines and propositions.

In the end, however, the truth about our infinite God is beyond human understanding and expression. As Paul exclaimed, "How unsearchable are His judgments and His ways past finding out!" (Romans 11:33). Sometimes all we can do is praise our Lord for His greatness with our words and with our songs (Psalm 150:2).

The psalmist talked about using all kinds of instruments in praise and worship of the Lord (vv. 3–5). We too use hymns, choruses, cantatas, organs, pianos, orchestras, and every available form of music to convey our adoration of the God "who alone has immortality, dwelling in unapproachable light" (1 Timothy 6:16).

God has revealed himself so we can know Him and the salvation He provides. But we will never understand the depth of His being. He is worthy of all praise!

—*Vernon Grounds*

Backstory

The theologian in question in this story is Karl Barth, and the truthfulness of the story has been verified by people who were at the event when he made the statement.

REFRAIN

The ways to praise God are as numerous as there are styles of music and varieties of instruments.

The Danger of Denial

From God's Hymnal: John 18:12–27

If we endure, we shall also reign with Him. If we deny Him, He also will deny us.
—2 TIMOTHY 2:12

We usually think that denying Christ is an outright act—like Peter's disavowal of Jesus in John 18. But Reginald Heber (1783–1826), the English writer of the hymn "Holy, Holy, Holy," pointed out that we can deny the Savior in more subtle ways.

Heber wrote: "We deny our Lord whenever, like Demas, we, through love of this present world, forsake the course of duty which Christ has plainly pointed out to us. We deny our Lord whenever we lend . . . our praise, or even our silence, to [things] . . . which we ourselves believe to be sinful. . . . We deny our Lord whenever we forsake a good man in affliction, and refuse to give countenance, encouragement, and support to those who, for God's sake and for the faithful discharge of their duty, are exposed to persecutions and slander."

Those who have been born again will consciously avoid any open, deliberate, and vocal denial of the Lord. But loving the world, failing to do as God directs, tolerating sin, and refusing to support our fellow believers are subtle ways we do, in effect, deny the One who has redeemed us.

Let's determine to live faithfully for Jesus so that no one will ever be able to accuse us of turning our backs on Him. Remember, we're always in danger of denial.

—*Richard DeHaan*

 REFRAIN

Allegiance to our Lord should be one of our top priorities—and the proof of our allegiance stems from what we say and do to honor Him.

One Tongue Is Enough

From God's Hymnal: Psalm 45

My tongue is the pen of a ready writer. —Psalm 45:1

All of us as Christians who long to proclaim the riches of Christ and His good news know the limitations of having only one tongue. In one of his hymns, Charles Wesley (1707–1788) wrote, "O for a thousand tongues to sing my great Redeemer's praise!"

The fact is, though, that our one tongue has vastly greater potential than most of us will ever put to use. A tongue devoted to God can accomplish much.

Backstory

Charles Wesley wrote 6,000 hymns during his lifetime. He wrote "O for a Thousand Tongues" in 1739. During his years of writing, he tried to pen three hymns a week.

For example, a man from Chicago was blind and had neither arms nor legs. But like the psalmist, his heart was overflowing with God's love, and his tongue was fully dedicated for His use. This man learned to read the Braille Bible using his tongue! As a result of this painstaking accomplishment, he was able to use his tongue in a different way—to teach the Word of God and to share his radiant testimony.

Joni Eareckson Tada, another believer with physical disabilities, has spoken to millions about Christ. She often affirms, "With God, less is more."

Are you sometimes discouraged, thinking that you have little to offer to God? If you have Christ's love in your heart and a willing tongue in your mouth, offer them boldly to God today and begin to bring praise and honor to the Lord. One tongue is enough.

—*Joanie Yoder*

♪ Refrain

Perhaps the reason one tongue doesn't seem enough to praise God is that we sometimes spend too much time allowing our tongue to speak negatively of others.

The Witness of Suffering

From God's Hymnal: Acts 7:54–8:4

Those who are scattered went everywhere preaching the word. —ACTS 8:4

A brilliant philosopher and theologian made this strong statement: "No one was ever saved by apologetics." He wasn't downplaying the importance of being ready to give reasons for our faith. But persuasive arguments aren't enough. People must choose for themselves to believe in Jesus.

How do we lead them to choose Christ? The use of logic is one way. But we will probably get a lot further by living an active, unwavering faith before them.

Consider the witness we give when we are faithful through suffering. My mind is drawn to Annie Johnson Flint, author of thousands of hymns and gospel songs. Her birth parents died when she was very young. She lived with crippling arthritis. She was stricken with cancer. Yet her faith was especially evident in this hymn:

Backstory

Annie Johnson Flint spent most of her adult life in a sanatorium as she battled debilitating arthritis. A teacher by profession, she had to give that up because of her physical disabilities.

> *He giveth more grace when the burdens grow greater,*
> *He sendeth more strength when the labors increase;*
> *To added afflictions He addeth His mercy,*
> *To multiplied trials His multiplied peace.*

God has a remarkable way of using negative circumstances to bring about good. The persecution of the early church, while intended to stamp out the gospel, actually resulted in its rapid growth (Acts 8:4). And though no one would call the suffering of Annie Johnson Flint a good thing, her faithfulness through trials was a wonderful witness to God's grace.

May our faithfulness in the midst of suffering be used to deliver a powerful witness for Christ.

—*David Egner*

REFRAIN

One of the best arguments we can give others regarding our faith is that God is faithful during the hard times.

Safe in God's Care

From God's Hymnal: Acts 27:27–44

The LORD shall preserve your going out and your coming in from this time forth, and even forevermore. —PSALM 121:8

President Franklin D. Roosevelt loved the song we call the "Navy Hymn." It was sung at his funeral in Hyde Park, New York, on April 14, 1945. The words of the hymn were written in 1860 by Englishman William Whiting, who taught and directed a sixteen-voice boys choir. He penned them for a student who was about to set sail for America and who was apprehensive about the journey.

The beautiful tune was written by John B. Dykes and first published in 1861. He named the hymn tune "Melita," the Roman name for Malta, the island where Paul was shipwrecked.

The hymn is a simple prayer based on the profound truth that the eternal God who created the universe controls all the elements of nature and can protect His own no matter how great the peril. Wind and wave are subject to His command. The first verse reads:

> *Eternal Father, strong to save,*
> *Whose arm doth bind the restless wave,*
> *Who bidd'st the mighty ocean deep*
> *Its own appointed limits keep;*
> *O hear us when we cry to Thee*
> *For those in peril on the sea!*

Backstory

In 1879, Rear Admiral Charles Jackson Train began the tradition of ending the worship service on Sunday at the US Naval Academy with a singing of the first verse of the "Navy Hymn."

When we or loved ones take a journey to some far-off destination, or if we only travel to and from work, we can think of these famous words from this widely respected hymn and be sure of God's protection and care.

—David Egner

REFRAIN

How can we go into any adventure with more courage than to ask God to be with us "wheresoe'er [we] go" as the "Navy Hymn" proclaims?

Grandpa's Last Hymn

From God's Hymnal: Matthew 26:17–30

When they had sung a hymn, they went out to the Mount of Olives.
—Matthew 26:30

As our Lord faced the terrible prospect of dying on the cross, He concluded the first Communion service with the singing of a hymn. By this He showed that believers can meet the "last enemy" with peaceful confidence when they have faith in God and His sustaining grace.

I remember hearing my parents telling about Grandpa Bosch's final moments on this earth. He had become afflicted with a serious heart ailment, and in spite of the doctor's best efforts to relieve his condition he steadily worsened. After three trying days and nights, he realized that death was near.

Calling his children to his side, he lovingly spoke to each of them. Then he said, "Let's part with a hymn." His weak voice quavered as he sang these familiar words by Edward Mote:

> *My hope is built on nothing less*
> *Than Jesus' blood and righteousness.*
> *His oath, His covenant, His blood,*
> *Support me in the whelming flood.*
> *When all around my soul gives way,*
> *He then is all my hope and stay.*
> *On Christ, the solid Rock, I stand,*
> *All other ground is sinking sand.*

After a tender word of spiritual admonition, Grandpa closed his eyes and went to be with the Lord.

If we rely on Christ, we too will have that kind of peace when we come to the end of our lives.

—Henry Bosch

 Refrain

When all of life gives way and there is but one thing left to consider, may Jesus Christ and His sacrifice for us be our sole concern.

Always Available

From God's Hymnal: 2 Corinthians 12:7–10

I can do all things through Christ who strengthens me. —PHILIPPIANS 4:13

Swedish hymnist Lina Sandell Berg (1832–1903) served with her father in an evangelistic ministry. As they were traveling by boat across Lake Vattern in their homeland, he accidentally fell overboard and drowned. In need of the comfort that only God can supply, Lina wrote the following words that are still sung by Christians around the world:

> *Day by day and with each passing moment,*
> *Strength I find to meet my trials here;*
> *Trusting in my Father's wise bestowment,*
> *I've no cause for worry or for fear.*

Secular counselors advise us to draw strength from our own inner resources. But that's hopelessly unrealistic. The simple fact is that in and of ourselves we don't have what it takes to deal with all of life's pressures and problems. Even the strongest among us have weaknesses. We're susceptible to vacillating moods, sinful temptations, and enslaving habits.

In 2 Corinthians 12:7–10, the apostle Paul referred to a weakness he called a "thorn in the flesh." But he didn't tough it out on his own. He prayed for deliverance, but instead of getting that, he was strengthened by the Lord so he could endure his overwhelming difficulties.

Backstory

It has been noted that this and other songs Lina wrote following her father's death were instrumental in fueling a revival that touched thousands of lives in Scandinavia in the later half of the nineteenth century.

In times of conflict and defeat, we are forced to confess that we need a source of strength beyond ourselves. And we can rejoice that there's an always-available source on which we can draw—the inexhaustible grace of God.

—*Vernon Grounds*

⚘ REFRAIN

Our inner strength is sometimes small during our times of greatest need; God's strength is great when we need it most.

Church Competition

From God's Hymnal: Philippians 1:12–18

Whether in pretense or in truth, Christ is preached; and in this I rejoice.
—PHILIPPIANS 1:18

Three churches, located on different corners of the same intersection, didn't get along. One Sunday each of them opened their meeting with a rousing song service. It was a warm day and all the doors and windows were wide open. One congregation began singing the old hymn, "Will There Be Any Stars in My Crown?" The strains had barely faded away when the congregation across the street started singing, "No, Not One, No, Not One!" They had scarcely finished when the third church began singing, "Oh, That Will Be Glory for Me."

Of course, this is just a humorous story, but it reminds us that a spirit of divisive competition does exist among some churches. Naturally, we will want to support our own church, pray for it, and rejoice in its growth. But we must never feel self-satisfied or be critical of churches that have problems or are not growing.

If there is a place for "competition," let it be to oppose those who deny scriptural fundamentals and the gospel. But if a church is true to God's Word and is winning people to Christ, regardless of its label, let's rejoice. That should be our attitude when faced with the competitive motives of envy and strife. Let's avoid church competition.

—*Richard DeHaan*

Backstory

The song "Oh, That Will Be Glory for Me" is sometimes called the "Glory Song." It has faced criticism from some because of its overemphasis on the believer's heavenly reward bringing glory to us instead of to God.

REFRAIN

Our joy must be that Jesus Christ is honored and glorified, not that our specific group of believers receives recognition.

Tell It to Jesus

From God's Hymnal: Matthew 14:1–12

[John's] disciples came and took away the body [of John] and buried it, and went and told Jesus. —MATTHEW 14:12

When I was a young boy, a neighbor who lived two doors from us suffered a terrible tragedy. She often played and sang at her piano, but after her great sorrow the first song she always sang when she sat down to play was "I Must Tell Jesus." The words of that lovely old hymn made a deep impression on me.

What comfort in those words:

> *I must tell Jesus all of my troubles,*
> *He is a kind, compassionate Friend;*
> *If I but ask Him, He will deliver,*
> *Make of my troubles quickly an end.*
> *I must tell Jesus! I must tell Jesus!*
> *I cannot bear these burdens alone;*
> *I must tell Jesus! I must tell Jesus!*
> *Jesus can help me, Jesus alone.*

I learned later that God answered our neighbor's prayers in such unusual ways that out of her sorrows came great blessings. Apparently, Jesus had become more real to her than He had ever been before her terrible tragedy.

Matthew said that after John the Baptist was beheaded his disciples "took away the body and buried it" (14:12). The record is strangely silent about any sorrow, but the last part of the verse says it all. Matthew wrote that they "went and told Jesus." It seemed the only thing to do.

Are you heavy-hearted? Tell it to Jesus!

—*Henry Bosch*

Backstory

Pastor Elisha Hoffman (see "Everlasting Arms") visited a parishioner who faced many struggles. She asked Pastor Hoffman what to do, and he said she should tell Jesus her troubles. She responded, "I must tell Jesus, I must tell Jesus." Later that day, with those words in his head, Hoffman wrote the song.

♪ REFRAIN

Our burdens may be too heavy for us to carry, but Jesus has told us we can cast them on Him. What's stopping us?

Just As You Are

From God's Hymnal: Titus 2:11–3:5

For by grace you have been saved through faith, and that not of yourselves; it is the gift of God, not of works, lest anyone should boast. —Ephesians 2:8–9

I read a story about Cesar Malan (1787–1864), a famous minister from Geneva, Switzerland, who had a genuine interest in the spiritual welfare of anyone with whom he came in contact. On one occasion, after being introduced to a woman, Malan asked his new acquaintance about her personal relationship with the Lord. Caught off guard, and somewhat annoyed by his question, she curtly said that she didn't care to discuss the matter. The minister kindly assured her that he would be praying for her salvation.

It wasn't long before circumstances brought the two together again. As they talked, it became apparent to Pastor Malan that his prayers were being answered. The once antagonistic woman had recognized her spiritual need and was now asking him what was required to come to the Savior. The preacher replied, "Come to Him just as you are." And that's what she did. Realizing that she could do nothing to save herself and depending on the finished work of Christ on the cross to pay for her sins, she received Him by faith as her Savior. That woman was Charlotte Elliott, who later wrote the beloved hymn, "Just As I Am."

All who desire to be saved must come to the Lord Jesus the same way she did. Admitting their sinfulness, and believing that Christ died for them, they must trust Him and Him alone for their salvation. Have you ever done that? If not, right now make the words of Charlotte Elliott your prayer.

—*Richard DeHaan*

Backstory

Cesar Malan was a Renaissance man, of sorts, not long after the Renaissance. He was a pastor, a songwriter, a writer, an artist, and a mechanic. But most of all, he loved to share the gospel.

REFRAIN

If Jesus had not died, we would have to try to change ourselves. But because of His sacrifice, He can take us just as we are and transform us.

"Just As I Am"

From God's Hymnal: John 6:35–40

All that the Father gives Me will come to Me, and the one who comes to Me I will by no means cast out. —John 6:37

Charlotte Elliott (1789–1871) learned an important lesson about Jesus one sleepless night in 1834. Some time after her salvation (see "Just As You Are"), she became disabled and was unable to attend when her family held a bazaar in Brighton, England, to raise money to build a school.

That night she was overwhelmed by her inability to help, and she could not sleep. But her sadness was turned to joy when she recalled that God accepted her just as she was.

That experience inspired her to write these well-loved words:

> Just as I am, without one plea
> But that Thy blood was shed for me,
> And that Thou bidd'st me come to Thee,
> O Lamb of God, I come! I come!

Backstory

Charlotte Elliott wrote "Just As I Am" when she was 45 years old, and the words were first published in 1836. The music we associate with the hymn was written in 1849 by William B. Bradbury (1816–1868).

When she published the poem in *The Invalid's Hymn Book*, she paired John 6:37 with it.

Jesus always accepts people as they are. In John 6, the people had come from miles around to hear Jesus. When the crowd became hungry, He miraculously fed them with a boy's unselfish gift of five loaves and two fish. Then the Lord offered himself as "the bread of life," promising that He would not turn away anyone who came to Him.

It's still true today. No one who comes to Jesus will be turned away. Come to Him with all your sin—just as you are. Our Savior's salvation, purchased with His death on the cross, can make you just as you should be.

—*David Egner*

♪ REFRAIN

While "Just As I Am" is how we come to Jesus, He does not leave us as we are. He transforms us through His love and forgiveness.

Fruit—After Many Days!

From God's Hymnal: Ecclesiastes 11:1–6

He shall be like a tree planted by the rivers of water, that brings forth its fruit in its season, whose leaf also shall not wither; and whatever he does shall prosper.
—Psalm 1:3

In the previous two devotions, you read the story of how Charlotte Elliott came to write her heart-searching hymn "Just As I Am." Miss Elliott suffered intense pain in her bedridden condition, and she was seldom permitted a visitor. Those who looked at her life may have thought it was wasted, but after her death, friends found in an old trunk more than 1,000 letters that had come to her from all over the world, thanking her for the courage, inspiration, and comfort her one simple invitation song had brought to them.

Like a well-watered tree of the Lord, she had done His bidding and brought forth "much fruit," although it was not until "after many days" that it became evident how much the Lord had prospered her in penning her beloved and immortal hymn.

I am sure that someday many more thousands will testify in glory that "Just As I Am" was used of the Lord to bring the conviction of heart and understanding of mind that was needed to usher them into the kingdom of God!

If our "leaf of testimony" does not wither, we, like Charlotte Elliott, will "bring forth . . . fruit" in God's appointed "season"—even though it may be after many days!

—*Henry Bosch*

Backstory

William B. Bradbury, who wrote the music for Charlotte's "Just As I Am," also wrote the tunes that accompany "He Leadeth Me," "Sweet Hour of Prayer," and "Savior, Like a Shepherd Lead Us."

 REFRAIN

We plant the seeds in our time; God provides the fruit in His.

"O Yes, He Cares"

From God's Hymnal: Luke 12:22–30

Casting all your care upon Him, for He cares for you. —1 PETER 5:7

Sometimes Christians wonder if God really cares. These periods of questioning usually do not arise during happier times. Instead, they occur when the burdens of life weigh heavily, when temptation has been overpowering, or when a final farewell must be said. Yet our text for today says the Lord Jesus cares so much that He will always be with us to help.

A hymn on this theme, "Does Jesus Care?" by Frank E. Graeff (1860–1919), has brought comfort to thousands. In his book *101 More Hymn Stories*, Kenneth Osbeck wrote, "Mr. Graeff was a pastor in the Philadelphia area. Throughout the district, he was known as 'the sunshine minister.' C. Austin Miles, author of the popular hymn, 'In the Garden,' paid this tribute to Mr. Graeff: 'He is a spiritual optimist, a great friend of children; his bright sun-shining disposition attracts him not only to children, but to all with whom he comes in contact. He has a holy magnetism and a childlike faith.' In spite of his cheery disposition and winsome personality, Graeff was often called upon to go through severe testing experiences." While enduring one such test—he faced severe despondency, doubt, and physical agony—Graeff turned to the Scriptures for solace and strength. The words of 1 Peter 5:7, "He cares for you," spoke deeply to him, and the hymn "Does Jesus Care?" was born.

Is your heart filled with pain or grief? Read 1 Peter 5:7 and remind yourself, "O yes, He cares!"

—*David Egner*

> ## Backstory
>
> Frank E. Graeff was not just a songwriter (200 songs) and a pastor; he was also a novelist. His book was called *The Minister's Twins*.

REFRAIN

"When the days are weary, the long nights dreary, I know my Savior cares." *Graeff*

"Abide with Me"... and Soccer?

From God's Hymnal: Hebrews 13:1–8

Let your conduct be without covetousness; be content with such things as you have. For He Himself has said, "I will never leave you nor forsake you." —Hebrews 13:5

One of the highlights of English football (soccer) each year is the final match of the annual FA Cup Final. For more than a hundred years, the day has been marked by excitement, festivity, and competition. But what fascinates me is how the game begins. It starts with the singing of Henry Lyte's traditional hymn "Abide with Me."

At first that struck me as odd. What does that hymn have to do with football? As I thought about it, though, I realized that for the follower of Christ it has everything to do with sports, shopping, working, going to school, or anything else we do. Since there is no corner of our lives that should not be affected by the presence of God, the longing that He would abide with us is actually the most reasonable thing we could desire. Of course, the presence of our heavenly Father is not something we need to plead for—it is promised to us. In Hebrews 13:5, we read, "For [God] Himself has said, 'I will never leave you nor forsake you.'"

Not only is God's presence the key to our contentment, but it is also the promise that can give us wisdom, peace, comfort, and strength—no matter where we are or what we are doing.

—Bill Crowder

Backstory

One of the most stirring renditions of "Abide with Me" in an English football venue is one by Hayley Westenra of New Zealand as she leads the crowd in this time-honored song. You can probably find it on YouTube.

REFRAIN

There is no situation unusual enough to conclude that God will not be with you and guide you to live for Him, serve Him, and honor Him.

His Love, Not Ours

From God's Hymnal: 1 John 4:7–16

Therefore the sisters sent to Him, saying, "Lord, behold, he whom You love is sick." —JOHN 11:3

When a godly Christian became seriously ill, several friends gathered around his bedside to ask God to restore him. The last one to pray spoke of the faithful service of this man and concluded his petition by saying, "Lord, You know how he loves You." After a moment of silence, the sick believer said to him, "I know you meant well, but please don't plead for my recovery on that basis. When Lazarus was ill, Mary and Martha sent for Jesus, but their request was not based on his affection for Christ. They said, 'Lord, he whom You love is sick.' It's not my weak and faltering allegiance to Him that calls forth His attention but His perfect love for me that is my constant strength and hope."

The same thought was forcefully impressed on hymn writer Philip P. Bliss one day after he finished singing "Oh, How I Love Jesus." "These words are true," he said. "Yet I feel guilty for having sung so much about my poor love for Christ and so little about His endless love for me." As a result, he wrote a song that is well known today. It reads,

> *I am so glad that our Father in heaven*
> *Tells of His love in the Book He has given,*
> *Wonderful things in the Bible I see—*
> *This is the dearest, that Jesus loves me.*

Yes, our greatest comfort in life or in death is not that we love Him, but that "He loved us" (1 John 4:10).

—*Henry Bosch*

Backstory

Philip P. Bliss died at the age of 38 while traveling by train near Ashtabula, Ohio. He and his wife, Lucy, both died when a bridge collapsed and the train in which they were riding crashed into a ravine on December 29, 1876.

REFRAIN

Of all the words the English language can give us, perhaps the greatest three are these: "Jesus loves me."

One Last Song

From God's Hymnal: Hebrews 13:7–17

*Let your conduct be without covetousness; be content with such things as you have. For He Himself has said, "I will never leave you nor forsake you." —*Hebrews 13:5

In life and in death, one mark that should distinguish the Christian from those who do not know the Savior is praise to God. Even when our dearest treasures are taken from us, the Father reassures us that we are His children, heirs together with Christ (Romans 8:17).

Renowned pastor Louis Albert Banks (1855–1933) tells of an elderly Christian man, a fine singer, who learned that he had cancer of the tongue and that surgery was required. In the hospital after everything was ready for the operation, the man asked the doctor, "Do you think I will ever sing again?" The surgeon found it difficult to answer his question. He simply shook his head no. The patient then asked if he could sit up for a moment. "I've had many good times singing the praises of God," he said. "And now you tell me I can never sing again. I have one song that will be my last. It will be of gratitude and praise to God." There in the doctor's presence the man sang softly the words of Isaac Watts' hymn,

> I'll praise my Maker while I've breath,
> And when my voice is lost in death,
> Praise shall employ my nobler powers;
> My days of praise shall ne'er be past,
> While life, and thought, and being last,
> Or immortality endures.

Backstory

According to the journal of well-known eighteenth-century theologian John Wesley, in an entry written "by one who was present," this was also the last song he sang. While on his deathbed in March 1791, he sang Isaac Watts' hymn.

Praise in times of trial isn't natural—it's the supernatural work of the Holy Spirit in the heart of an obedient believer.

—*Dennis DeHaan*

♪ REFRAIN

How grand it would be if the last song on our lips would be one in which we say, "I'll praise my Maker while I've breath."

"Jesus, Savior, Pilot Me"

From God's Hymnal: Matthew 8:23–27

He calms the storm, so that its waves are still. Then they are glad because they are quiet; so He guides them to their desired haven. —Psalm 107:29–30

One of the most vivid pictures of the Christian's journey through life is that of a voyage on a storm-tossed sea. Edward Hopper (1818–1888) captured this theme in his well-loved hymn "Jesus, Savior, Pilot Me." Born and raised on America's East Coast, he knew much about the sea. For 17 years he pastored a church that was originally established as a mission for sailors and fishermen. Hopper loved these men and was intrigued by their accounts of harrowing experiences during storms and high winds. After preaching one Sunday from Matthew 8, the account of Jesus calming the boisterous Sea of Galilee, he felt inspired to write the words of his now famous hymn. The last stanza is beautiful in its simplicity and directness. It reads,

When at last I near the shore,
And the fearful breakers roar
'Twixt me and the peaceful rest—
Then, while leaning on Thy breast,
May I hear Thee say to me, "Fear not—
I will pilot thee!"

Several years after writing that song, he composed another bit of verse about heaven. After Hopper died, he was found in his study chair, pencil still in hand—with that unfinished poem about heaven on the paper in front of him.

Friend, only when Jesus is at the helm of your life will you arrive safely at the "desired haven" of heaven.

—*Henry Bosch*

♪ REFRAIN

In both the high winds and storms of life and in the calmer days of pleasant breezes, we need the help and guidance of our pilot, Jesus.

Glory in the Cross!

From God's Hymnal: John 19:16–30

God forbid that I should boast except in the cross of our Lord Jesus Christ, by whom the world has been crucified to me, and I to the world. —GALATIANS 6:14

Many years ago, at a gospel meeting in the Grand Rapids (MI) Civic Auditorium, I was privileged to hear George Bennard sing "The Old Rugged Cross." He was a short, rather slightly built man with white wavy hair and a face that shone with the love of God. Before singing that favorite of all hymns, he told the audience that the inspiration to write it came to him one day in 1913. He said, "After composing the melody, the words were put into my heart in answer to my own need in a time of crisis. I had come to realize that the cross is more than just a religious symbol. Along with the resurrection, it is at the very heart of the gospel."

Following that brief introduction, Mr. Bennard sang "The Old Rugged Cross" as I had never heard it rendered before. His face appeared radiant with the glory of God as he sang,

> *O that old rugged cross, so despised by the world,*
> *Has a wondrous attraction for me;*
> *For the dear Lamb of God left His glory above*
> *To bear it to dark Calvary.*
> *To the old rugged cross I will ever be true,*
> *Its shame and reproach gladly bear;*
> *Then He'll call me someday to my home far away,*
> *Where His glory forever I'll share.*

Backstory

The first time the completed version of "The Old Rugged Cross" was sung, on June 7, 1913, it was accompanied with a guitar. Reed City, Michigan, where Bennard lived, is the home of the Old Rugged Cross Historical Museum.

May we never be ashamed of what Jesus did for us. Let us glory in that old rugged cross, where the "dearest and best" suffered and died for unworthy rebels like you and me.

—*Henry Bosch*

♪ REFRAIN

It's not a new concept that the cross is "despised by the world" as Bennard wrote over 100 years ago. But that should never stop us from cherishing the cross and our Savior who died on it.

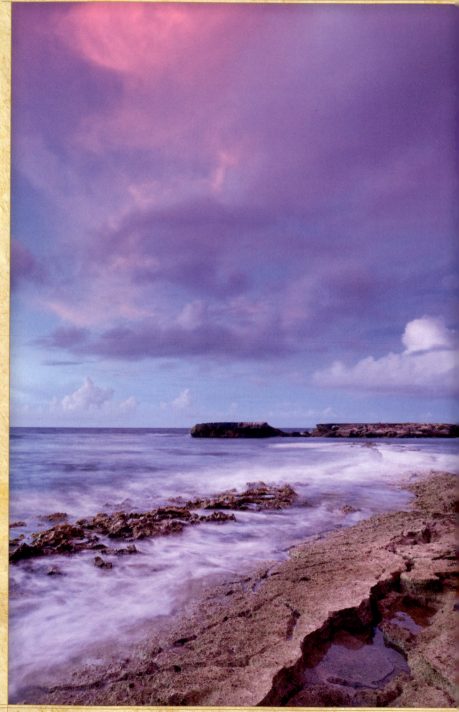

A Great and Grand Reunion

From God's Hymnal: 1 Thessalonians 4:13–18

We who are alive and remain shall be caught up together with them in the clouds to meet the Lord in the air. —1 Thessalonians 4:17

In a sermon about heaven, evangelist D. L. Moody (1837–1899) told about the brave fishermen who ventured far out upon the Adriatic Sea off the east coast of Italy. Toward evening their wives would go down to the seashore to await the joyous reunion with their husbands. Standing there, they would sing the first verse of a beautiful hymn. Then they would stop to listen till they heard the second verse, carried by the wind across the waves, sung by those courageous men. With wishful thinking, Moody would continue, "Perhaps if we would listen, we too might hear some sound, some whisper borne from loved ones afar." Of course, Moody knew that Christians who die are "present with the Lord" (2 Corinthians 5:8). Yet, as he contemplated being united with them someday, he said he could almost hear the echo of their voices "breaking in music upon the sands of time."

Most of us have dear ones in heaven. I like to think that even as we long to see them, they are eagerly awaiting that day when we'll all be together again. No doubt Fanny Crosby had this in mind when she wrote:

> O the friends that now are waiting, in the cloudless realms of day,
> Who are calling me to follow where their steps have led the way;
> I shall see them, I shall know them, I shall hear their song of love,
> And we'll all sing hallelujah in our Father's house above.

As we think of our loved ones on that heavenly shore, let's rejoice! One of these days we're going to have a great and grand reunion.

—*Richard DeHaan*

Backstory

Interestingly, Fanny Crosby, who was blind from infancy, entitled the song mentioned above "The Blessed Lights of Home." Charles H. Marsh (1886–1956) wrote the music for Miss Crosby's words.

REFRAIN

The days of sighing and sadness on earth will someday be replaced with moments of rejoicing and gladness in heaven.

"Nearer, My God, to Thee"

From God's Hymnal: James 4:1–8

*Draw near to God and He will draw near to you. Cleanse your hands, you sinners;
and purify your hearts, you double-minded.* —James 4:8

In his interesting book *Singing with Understanding*, Kenneth Osbeck tells of the origin of the much-loved hymn "Nearer, My God, to Thee." Osbeck wrote that the author, Sarah Flower Adams (1805–1848) of England, was known for her literary talents. One day her pastor said he wished he could find a song to use with his sermon about the Lord's unique appearance to Jacob recorded in Genesis 28. In that passage Jacob was reminded of God's covenant of grace with him through a dream, which drew him into a closer fellowship with God. Having caught the gist of her minister's sermon, Sarah skillfully condensed that biblical story into five stanzas. These two give the spiritual flavor of its lyrics:

> *Nearer, my God, to Thee, nearer to Thee!*
> *E'en though it be a cross that raiseth me;*
> *Still all my song shall be, nearer, my God, to Thee.*
> *Nearer, my God, to Thee, nearer to Thee!*
> *There let the way appear, steps unto heaven;*
> *All that Thou sendest me, in mercy given—*
> *Angels to beckon me nearer, my God, to Thee.*

Backstory

The song "Nearer, My God, to Thee" was played at the funerals of US presidents James Garfield, Warren G. Harding, and Gerald R. Ford.

Many touching stories have been told of how this song was used in the hour of crisis. For instance, William McKinley, assassinated American president, whispered some of its words on his deathbed on September 14, 1901. And according to legend, in 1912 as the *Titanic* sank into the icy waters of the Atlantic sending 1,500 people into eternity, the band played, "Nearer, My God, to Thee."

The theme of this hymn ought to be our heart's desire today.

—Henry Bosch

REFRAIN

The nearer we draw to God, the farther away move the stumbling blocks and temptations of life.

Everyone Sings!

From God's Hymnal: Revelation 5:8–14

Blessing and honor and glory and power be to Him who sits on the throne, and to the Lamb, forever and ever! —REVELATION 5:13

Each summer I enjoy attending many of the free outdoor concerts presented in our city. During one performance by a brass band, several of the members briefly introduced themselves and told how much they enjoyed practicing and playing together.

The pleasure of sharing music in community has drawn people together for centuries. As followers of Christ, whether we are in small groups, choirs, or congregations, bringing praise to God is one of the key elements in our own expression of faith. And one day we'll be singing in a concert that defies imagination.

In a sweeping vision of the tumultuous events at the end of time, John records a chorus of praise that begins with a few saints and swells to a company beyond number. In honor of the Lamb of God, who with His blood has redeemed people from every tribe and nation (Revelation 5:9), the song begins at the throne of God, is joined by multiplied thousands of angels, and finally includes every creature in heaven, earth, and sea. Together we will sing, "Blessing and honor and glory and power be to Him who sits on the throne, and to the Lamb, forever and ever!" (v. 13).

What a choir! What a concert! What a privilege to start rehearsing today!

—*David McCasland*

Backstory

In *The Mesga* paraphrase, Revelation 19:1 reads: "I heard a sound like massed choirs in Heaven singing." It also says in Revelation 5: "I heard every creature in Heaven and earth, in underworld and sea, join in, all voices in all places, singing: To the One on the Throne! To the Lamb! (v. 13). There's lots of singing in heaven!

♪ REFRAIN

Think of it—the only specific activity that we know we can do here that we will do in heaven is to worship in song. Think of how vital that makes this activity!

We'll Sing and Shout!

From God's Hymnal: Revelation 21:1–5

The lepers are cleansed and the deaf hear. —Matthew 11:5

I was enjoying a concert by a singing group when I noticed what was happening in the front rows of the auditorium. A sign-language interpreter was gracefully communicating the words of each song to about twenty-five people who were deaf.

When the vocalists sang "Victory in Jesus," the man who was both the pianist and emcee asked the translator if her group would "sing" the chorus. She agreed, and he began to play. No voices were heard, but we sat in awe as her group joyfully expressed the words with their hands. Their faces beamed, reflecting the meaning of each phrase.

I glanced at the five vocalists on the stage. Their faces were fixed intently on that group of twenty-five as they "sang" about victory in Jesus and praising our Savior forever. It was a thrilling experience.

I couldn't help but think of what it will be like in heaven. The hearing impaired will be able to hear and sing. They will be part of the vast chorus of the redeemed as they join the angels in proclaiming the praises of the Most High God and of the Lamb.

A day of rejoicing awaits every believer in Jesus Christ. We'll all be transformed, glorified, made whole. When we all get to heaven, we'll "sing and shout the victory."

—*David Egner*

Backstory

The man who wrote "Victory in Jesus," Eugene Bartlett (1885–1941), was considered one of the key founders of the genre of Christian music called "Southern Gospel." He was inducted into the Gospel Music Hall of Fame in 1973. "Victory in Jesus" was the last of 800 songs Bartlett wrote in his life.

REFRAIN

As much as we enjoy the various victories we garner on earth, they cannot compare to the ultimate victory we will enjoy in heaven.

The Hymn That Blessed a Queen

From God's Hymnal: 1 Corinthians 10:1–4, 11

All drank the same spiritual drink. For they drank of that spiritual Rock that followed them, and that Rock was Christ. —1 Corinthians 10:4

At the time of her golden jubilee in June 1887, Queen Victoria of the United Kingdom received dignitaries from all over the world. Among those who came to honor her was a representative from Madagascar. After conveying the good wishes of his people, he surprised Her Majesty by asking permission to sing for her. Those assembled thought he would choose one of his country's native songs, but they were amazed when he began, "Rock of Ages, cleft for me, let me hide myself in Thee." The rendition was so beautiful that it brought tears to the eyes of the Queen.

The author of that grand hymn, Augustus Toplady, was saved at the age of sixteen while attending a small evangelistic meeting in a rural district of Ireland. The sermon, preached by an illiterate layman, pointed Augustus to the Lord Jesus Christ—the Rock of Ages—in whom he could hide from God's wrath and find peace and forgiveness. As the young convert became established in his new faith, he felt God's call and began studying for the ministry. Since he was very frail, however, his fiery zeal and inspired efforts soon put too much strain on his weak body. Yet his faith never wavered. Augustus Toplady died of tuberculosis when he was only thirty-eight, but the lyrics he wrote—"Rock of Ages," firmly based on the Scriptures—still live on!

The next time you sing that old favorite, notice how the truths of salvation are expressed in all the verses. They will bless you as they did the Queen of England so many years ago.

—*Henry Bosch*

Backstory

It has been noted by some that "Rock of Ages" was a favorite song of both Queen Victoria and of her husband, Prince Albert. According to author Robert D. Kalis, Prince Albert repeated the first stanza over and over while on his deathbed.

REFRAIN

At times we all need a place to hide—a place of solace and safety. For the child of God, the Rock of Ages is that place.

Lights On?

From God's Hymnal: Matthew 5:13–16

For you were once darkness, but now you are light in the Lord. Walk as children of light. —EPHESIANS 5:8

Jesus stressed the positive effect we can have on others when He said, "Let your light so shine before men, that they may see your good works and glorify your Father in heaven" (Matthew 5:16). But if sin dims our light, some we might have influenced for Christ may drift on in spiritual darkness.

Backstory

This story about the Lake Erie shipwreck came from a message by D. L. Moody, with whom Bliss was associated as a song leader. After Bliss heard the story, he wrote about the believer's responsibility to keep the "lower lights" burning to guide others to the safety of the Savior.

On a dark and stormy night with waves piling up like mountains on Lake Erie, a boat rocked and plunged near the Cleveland harbor. "Are we on course?" asked the captain, seeing only one beacon from the lighthouse. "Quite sure, sir," replied the officer at the helm. "Where are the lower lights?" "Gone out, sir." "Can we make the harbor?" "We must, or perish!" came the reply. With a steady hand and a stalwart heart, the officer headed the ship toward land. But in the darkness he missed the channel and the vessel was dashed to pieces on the rocks. Many lives were lost in a watery grave. This incident moved Philip P. Bliss to write the familiar hymn, "Let the Lower Lights Be Burning."

Jesus, the Light of the world, has gone to heaven. Now Christians have the responsibility to be the "lower lights" that guide sinners to the harbor of His redeeming grace.

How can we be sure that we are reflecting God's love to others? By voicing David's prayer, "Search me, O God, and . . . see if there is any wicked way in me" (Psalm 139:23–24). If we forsake sin, we can be certain our light is shining brightly in a dark and needy world.

—*Dennis DeHaan*

REFRAIN

If we ask God to point out the ways of right and wrong—instead of seeking the world's direction—His light will shine on our path.

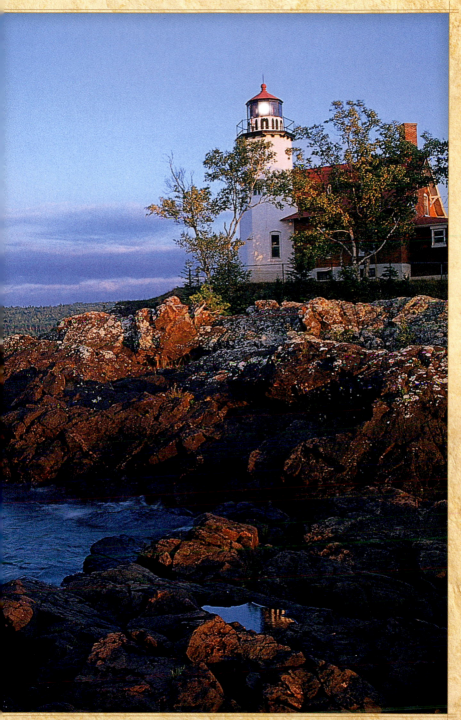

"God Will Take Care of You"

From God's Hymnal: Psalm 34:9–17

Then they cried out to the LORD in their trouble, and He saved them out of their distresses. —Psalm 107:13

In the early years of the twentieth century, Pastor W. Stillman Martin was in a perplexing situation. He was scheduled to preach in a distant town, yet he was worried about leaving home because his wife had unexpectedly become ill. After praying about his problem, he mentioned it to his children. One of them said, "Don't be afraid to go, Father. I'm sure God will take good care of Mother while you're away." The pastor remembered how he had often impressed upon them that they should put the Lord first in their lives and that they should keep their commitments. So casting aside his anxiety, he went in the confidence of Psalm 37:23, believing that the Lord was ordering his steps.

The services were richly blessed by God, and when he returned home, his wife was much improved. In gratitude to the Lord, Civilla Martin wrote a poem about God's loving help and providential care. Her husband improvised a melody on the organ to fit the words. It has become a famous and much-loved hymn:

> *Be not dismayed whate'er betide,*
> *God will take care of you;*
> *Beneath His wings of love abide,*
> *God will take care of you.*

Troubled believer, the Lord is interested in you and your problems. Call upon Him, and He will direct your steps and graciously take care of you.

—*Henry Bosch*

Backstory

One person who was helped greatly by Stillman and Civilla Martin's song was entrepreneur J. C. Penney. While recuperating from financially hard times, Penney entered a sanitarium in Michigan where he heard the song. This prompted him to visit the chapel on the grounds, and he turned his life back to God.

♪ REFRAIN

No matter what our circumstances or no matter where we travel, we cannot escape God's love and care.

Don't Forget to Crown Him!

From God's Hymnal: Romans 14:7–11

"But why do you call Me 'Lord, Lord,' and not do the things which I say?"
—Luke 6:46

Christ wants to be crowned king of our lives. We are to do more than call Him "Lord." We must allow Him to govern all our actions as well. Some of God's children are content to let Him save their souls but refuse to submit their bodies to Him as a living sacrifice (Romans 12:1–2).

A heartwarming story in the book *Forward Day by Day* tells about a song that especially delights youngsters. It's called, "Praise Him, All Ye Little Children." Sitting at the piano one day, a father and his young boy were singing it together. It is one of those gospel hymns that runs on and on with many satisfying but seemingly endless verses. They sang several stanzas:

> *Praise Him, praise Him, all ye little children,*
> *God is love, God is love . . .*
> *Love Him, love Him, all ye little children . . .*
> *Thank Him, thank Him, all ye little children . . .*
> *Serve Him, serve Him, all ye little children.*

Then the father stopped. The boy looked up in surprise, still expecting more. "Dad, you forgot to crown Him!" he said. And so once again they lifted their voices and sang, "Crown Him, crown Him, all ye little children; God is love, God is love!" Without realizing it, the child had emphasized a great biblical truth. As believers we say we love Christ and may even serve Him, but often we fail to give Him absolute control.

Jesus deserves your best, for He has bought you, soul and body. Don't forget to crown Him Lord of all!

—*Henry Bosch*

Backstory

Nobody knows who wrote the lyrics for "Praise Him, All Ye Little Children," but Carey Bonner wrote the music. He was a Baptist pastor from England and a pioneer in the growing Sunday school movement of the first part of the twentieth century.

♫ REFRAIN

In the never-ending song of our life, we could add "Worship Him," "Adore Him," "Honor Him," and many other stanzas.

"In the Sweet By and By"

From God's Hymnal: Romans 8:18–28

For I consider that the sufferings of this present time are not worthy to be compared with the glory which shall be revealed in us. —ROMANS 8:18

The gifted Christian musician Joseph P. Webster (1819–1875) was often tormented by deep feelings of depression. On one occasion when he was in a melancholy mood, he received a visit from his close acquaintance Sanford Bennett. Knowing that one way to help Webster was to interest him in writing a hymn tune, Bennett decided he'd try to pen some lyrics that would direct his friend's thoughts heavenward.

The despondent man himself unwittingly supplied the theme, for when he was asked, "What's the matter now?" he replied, "Oh, it will be all right by and by!" "That's true," exclaimed Bennett, "trials do generate great glory for us in the sweet by and by!" Bennett immediately sat down and wrote several poetic verses on the subject. When his friend read them, a new look of hope came into his eyes, and his whole attitude changed. After jotting down some musical notes, Webster took up his violin and played the melody he had composed to fit the words. The enduring hymn "In the Sweet By and By" was born.

It helped the musician see his trials in the light of heaven, for the lyrics read in part:

There's a land that is fairer than day, and by faith we can see it afar,
For the Father waits over the way to prepare us a dwelling-place there.
We shall sing on that beautiful shore the melodious songs of the blest;
And our spirits shall sorrow no more—not a sigh for the blessing of rest.

Yes, heaven's rewards will far outweigh earth's tears.

—*Henry Bosch*

Backstory

According to Sanford Bennett, it took no more than thirty minutes for Bennett and Joseph Webster to write both the words and music for this song. Bennett jotted the words down and turned them over to Webster, who quickly wrote the music.

REFRAIN

Sometimes the only thing that keeps us going in the here-and-now is the hope of what God has waiting for us in the by-and-by.

The Blind Carver's Hymn

From God's Hymnal: Psalm 55:1–6, 16–17

LORD, in trouble they have visited You, they poured out a prayer when Your chastening was upon them. —ISAIAH 26:16

Everyone in Coleshill, England, knew Bill Walford. During the week, he was forever whittling novelties for the children, and he managed to make a scant living by carving keepsake items and selling them in a little shop.

Walford was only a layman but was often asked to preach in different churches in his community. Although his life was filled with adversity, there was something uplifting about the elderly man's outlook on life.

One day in 1842 a minister named Thomas Salmon stopped in Walford's shop and found his friend occupied with more than his artistic carvings. He had a poem on prayer running through his mind and asked Salmon to take down the words as he recited them before they slipped from his memory. While he had rare spiritual insight, the reason Walford asked for help was that he was totally blind! Years later a copy of that verse came to the attention of a New York organist and composer William Bradbury. He immediately saw in Walford's poem the material for a comforting hymn, and in a short time wrote the tune.

You can live again that blind carver's spiritual emotions if you pay close attention to the words the next time you sing "Sweet Hour of Prayer."

—*Henry Bosch*

Backstory

One of the things Bill Walford did with his mind was to memorize large portions of Scripture. Some people in his community thought he might have memorized the entire Bible. "Sweet Hour of Prayer" was Walford's only verse ever put to music.

♪ REFRAIN

"Sweet hour of prayer, that calls me from a world of care and bids me at my Father's throne make all my wants and wishes known!"

The Making of Us

From God's Hymnal: Romans 8:18–29

For whom He foreknew, He also predestined to be conformed to the image of His Son, that He might be the firstborn among many brethren. —ROMANS 8:29

In a book by Robert V. Ozment entitled *But God Can*, some interesting observations are quoted from the Scottish author George MacDonald. Telling of a woman who had encountered a great tragedy in her life, he says, "The heartache was so crushing and her sorrow so bitter that the one in distress exclaimed, 'I wish I'd never been made.' With spiritual discernment, her friend answered, 'My dear, you are not fully made yet, you're only being made, and this is the Maker's process!'"

Someone has noted the apparent tragedies that became the making of the following men: "Milton, despite the blindness which overtook him, wrote the incomparable *Paradise Lost*. Beethoven became deaf but nevertheless wrote mighty music that made him famous.

"George Matheson went blind at college, but he refused to allow the calamity to frustrate his hopes. His majestic hymn 'O Love That Wilt Not Let Me Go' is a thing of beauty and a joy forever, and is universally sung throughout the world."

Does it seem as though everything in life is going against you? Have friends forsaken you, and are your dreams and aspirations shattered? Take heart! If you're a child of God, all things are working "for good." Rightly received, these experiences can truly be the making of you.

—*Richard DeHaan*

Backstory

George Matheson wrote "O Love . . ." in five minutes on the evening his sister was married. Apparently, her marriage reminded him of being rejected by his fiancée when he had gone blind some twenty years earlier. In his sadness, he wrote this song.

♪ REFRAIN

The beauty of our worst moments is that they can realign our attention and turn us toward the love of God—our only source of strength, hope, and true joy.

God's Unchanging Word

From God's Hymnal: 1 Peter 1:15–25

Forever, O LORD, Your word is settled in heaven. —PSALM 119:89

Henry Francis Lyte (1793–1847), the author of the well-known hymn "Abide with Me," lived more than 150 years ago, but his lyrics ring true today. Listen to his words:

> *Swift to its close ebbs out life's little day;*
> *Earth's joys grow dim, its glories pass away;*
> *Change and decay in all around I see—*
> *O Thou who changest not, abide with me.*

We live in an atmosphere of change. Today more than ever before, it appears that almost everything is in a state of flux. Very little seems to endure. Many well-established foundations are being shaken. The world is "on the move." As a result, this generation is restless, insecure, uncertain of who they are, why they are here, and where they are going. In such a day we should be thankful that there are some things that abide. First, we know a Person who never changes—One in whom we can place our trust and believe with all our hearts. We serve a God who is the same yesterday, today, and forever. He said, "I am the LORD, I do not change" (Malachi 3:6). There are also absolutes, principles, and abiding truths to guide and comfort us. These can be found in the Bible, the Word of God.

The psalmist declared, "Forever, O LORD, Your word is settled in heaven" (Psalm 119:89). Given to us by an immutable God, the Scriptures are His eternal truth. It is the message that groping, lost souls need today. Thank God for the Bible—His unchanging Word in a changing world!

—*Richard DeHaan*

Backstory

The writer of "Abide with Me," Henry Lyte, died from tuberculosis three weeks after penning this song.

🎵 REFRAIN

A world of constant change and turmoil calls for us to find peace and comfort in the One who never changes and who promises peace for our hearts.

The Cleansing Blood

From God's Hymnal: 1 John 1

If we walk in the light as He is in the light, we have fellowship with one another, and the blood of Jesus Christ His Son cleanses us from all sin. —1 JOHN 1:7

The hymns of Frances Ridley Havergal have greatly blessed the church. She wrote such songs as "Who Is on the Lord's Side?" "Like a River Glorious," "I Gave My Life for Thee," and "Take My Life and Let It Be." She was not always a happy Christian, however. As F. J. Huegel pointed out in his book *Forever Triumphant*, she was plagued by depression. Perhaps overly sensitive to faults in her life, she was a defeated believer who lacked the joy that should characterize every forgiven child of God. Huegel says, "She walked with bowed head. Romans 7 seemed to be her lot."

One day, though, she had a life-transforming experience. Huegel says that the Lord led her into the joy and blessing described in Romans 8. A great crisis marked Havergal's entrance into "the promised land of a life of fullness and victory." She was reading her New Testament in the Greek, as she often did. When she came to 1 John 1:7, she discovered from the tense of the verb that the blood of Christ *keeps on* cleansing the believer who walks in the light. Says Huegel, "The result for Frances Havergal was a mighty revolution. A new day dawned. She would no longer be sad because of her faults and blemishes. She would rejoice because of the infinite efficacy of the Savior's atoning death."

As we journey through this sinful world, we become defiled. But thank God, the blood of Jesus Christ keeps on cleansing us from all sin.

—*Richard DeHaan*

Backstory

Not only did Frances Havergal read Greek, but she also learned Latin and Hebrew. She memorized the Psalms, Isaiah, and most of the New Testament during her 43 years of life. The verse in this story (1 John 1:7) was engraved on her tombstone in Swansea, Wales.

 REFRAIN

A full and victorious life can be enjoyed by those who recognize the ongoing, continual cleansing Jesus gives us from sin.

Heart Music

From God's Hymnal: Psalm 98

Let the word of Christ dwell in you richly in all wisdom, teaching and admonishing one another in psalms and hymns and spiritual songs, singing with grace in your hearts to the Lord. —Colossians 3:16

Some good questions to ask yourself before the next song service begins at church are these: Do I really mean what I'm singing? Is this coming from my heart, or am I just going through the motions?

We sing, "'Tis the Blessed Hour of Prayer" and then allow our thoughts to wander aimlessly while we or others pray. We plead with enthusiam, "Bring Them In" and later gripe about the repeated call for people to do outreach. We sing, "For the Beauty of the Earth" and then pollute it with garbage. We raise our voices to ask, "Is It the Crowning Day?" and then live as though we had never heard of the Savior's return. We love the hymn, "Holy Bible, Book Divine" but spend most of our time reading novels and poring over websites. We sing, "I Love to Tell the Story" and can't remember the last time we spoke a word for Christ. We sing, "Just One Step at a Time" and immediately begin to worry about tomorrow!

This is not singing from our hearts. Someone has observed that "when the heart moves devoutly with the voice, true heart-singing results." I would add that it is whenever "the heart and hand move devoutly with the voice." Our devotion is shown by what we sing and do. When our songs are matched by our deeds—this is heart music!

—*Richard DeHaan*

Backstory

Folliott S. Pierpoint (1835–1917), who wrote the song "For the Beauty of the Earth," was overwhelmed by the natural magnificence of his region in England near the town of Bath. The region's limestone hills have been labeled an Area of Outstanding Natural Beauty. Pierpoint was both a teacher and a poet.

♪ REFRAIN

Knowing a song by heart and taking a song to heart are two different things. Our devotion to the Lord comes through when we allow a song to change our heart in praise and glory to God.

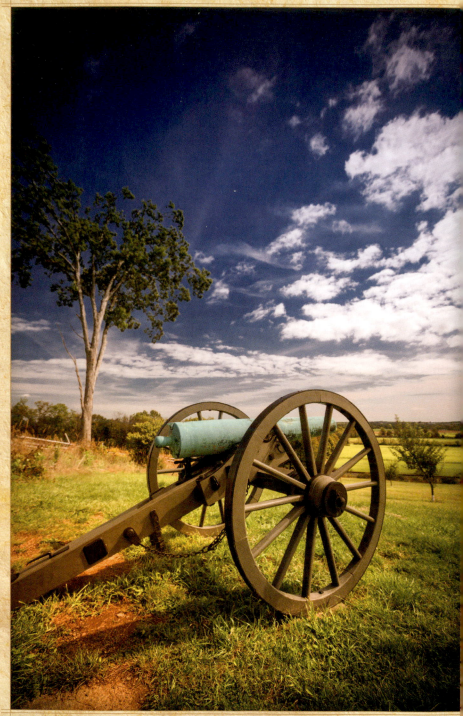

Hold the Fort

From God's Hymnal: Revelation 2:25–29

But hold fast what you have till I come. —Revelation 2:25

One of the favorite hymns of my father, Dr. M. R. DeHaan, was "Hold the Fort." Deeply aware of the spiritual battle in which we as believers are engaged, and eagerly looking for the coming of the Lord, how he loved to sing:

> *See the mighty hosts advancing, Satan leading on;*
> *mighty men around us falling, courage almost gone!*
> *"Hold the fort, for I am coming," Jesus signals still.*
> *Wave the answer back to heaven, "By Thy grace we will."*

In his book *Moody's Anecdotes*, J. B. McClure related this story: "When General Sherman went through Atlanta toward the sea in the Civil War, he left in the fort, back in the Kennesaw Mountains, a handful of men to guard some rations. Confederate General Hood, however, attacked the fort. Half the defenders were either killed or badly hurt, and the general in command was wounded. When they were just about to surrender, Sherman got within 15 miles of the besieged camp, and, through the signal corps sent the message: 'Hold fast; we are coming. W. T. Sherman.' That message fired up the beleaguered troops, and they held out till reinforcements came. They kept the fort from the hands of the enemy."

Even as Sherman signaled, "Hold fast; I am coming," so our heavenly commander has given us the same challenge. One of the first messages sent from heaven after Christ's ascension was the assurance of His return (Acts 1:11). The Bible's last promise is from the lips of Jesus, who said, "Surely, I come quickly" (Revelation 22:20). With patience, courage, and hope, let's endure until the victory is won.

—*Richard DeHaan*

Backstory

Philip P. Bliss, who wrote the song "Hold the Fort," heard this story about General Sherman in 1870 during a Sunday school class.

♪ REFRAIN

Think of the areas in which we need to endure with the clear assurance that God's rescue is on the way. Then give those areas to the Lord with confidence.

Wherefore, Stand!

From God's Hymnal: Ephesians 6:10–18

Put on the whole armor of God, that you may be able to stand against the wiles of the devil. —EPHESIANS 6:11

In the year 1858 a great revival occurred in the city of Philadelphia. The godly evangelist was Dudley A. Tyng. At one meeting during the campaign, the crowd swelled to over 5,000 people. Pastor Tyng chose as his text Exodus 10:11, which reads, "Go now ye that are men, and serve the Lord." And during the message, he said he would rather lose his right arm than stop proclaiming God's Word. It was a soul-stirring sermon.

Backstory

After hearing Rev. George Duffield read his new poem, his Sunday school superintendent, Benedict Stewart, had a number of copies printed. Soon the song appeared in *The Sabbath Hymn Book* and it later became a favorite of Civil War soldiers.

A few days later, Tyng entered a barn where a mule was providing the power for a corn-shelling machine. The evangelist patted the animal on the neck with one hand, but the sleeve on his other arm got caught in the mechanism. The arm was badly mangled, and in a few hours Tyng died from loss of blood. Just before his death, however, he sent a message to the men who had been his associates in the revival work. "Tell them," he said, "to stand up for Jesus!" On the following Sunday, George Duffield preached at his own church taking for his text Ephesians 6:14, "Stand, therefore, having your loins girded about with truth, and having on the breastplate of righteousness." At the close of the message, he read a poem he had written embodying the dying words and sentiments of his departed friend Dudley Tyng. It was later set to a stirring tune and became the well-known hymn "Stand Up for Jesus."

One of the best ways for each of us to give glory and honor to our God is to "Stand up for Jesus."

— *Henry Bosch*

♪ REFRAIN

What does the term "Stand Up for Jesus" mean? It is a call to action—a reminder that we can best represent Jesus if we are willing to equip ourselves with the "whole armor of God."

Jonah on Board

From God's Hymnal: Jonah 1–2

Then the men were exceedingly afraid, and said to him, "Why have you done this?" For the men knew that he fled from the presence of the LORD, because he had told them. —JONAH 1:10

The year is 1748. A trading ship departs from an island off the west coast of Africa headed for England. Aboard is John Newton, a seaman with a reputation for profane language and ungodly living. As Newton later described it, the captain "would often tell me that to his grief he had a Jonah on board; that a curse attended me wherever I went, and that all the troubles he met with in the voyage were owing to his having taken me into the vessel."

The captain may have been right. Newton had earlier turned his back on God. But just as a storm had threatened to destroy the boat bearing Jonah, so too a fierce Atlantic wind rudely awakened John Newton. The vessel nearly broke apart. As the damaged ship drifted at sea, Newton prayed for God's mercy and put his faith in Jesus. That's how a blasphemous, disreputable seaman became, by God's grace, the godly penman of the words of the beloved hymn "Amazing Grace."

If you, like Jonah, are a child of God who has strayed or who has deliberately run away from the Lord, come home. Live for Him again. Or maybe you're like John Newton. You need to trust Jesus for salvation. Don't wait for one of life's storms to awaken you to your need. Turn to Christ today.

—*Dave Branon*

Backstory

Ironically, after he became a pastor, John Newton spoke to a congregation that included William Wilberforce and had some amount of influence on him. Wilberforce, of course, was a key figure in the move to abolish slavery in nineteenth-century England.

REFRAIN

You can never escape God's judgment nor flee His goodness.
In one way or another, we all must answer to Him.

Truly Amazing Grace!

From God's Hymnal: Ephesians 2:1–10

For by grace you have been saved through faith. —Ephesians 2:8
But by the grace of God I am what I am. —1 Corinthians 15:10

When Paul told the believers at Ephesus that salvation was by grace and not by works, he knew what he was talking about. If anyone had reason to boast of his religious accomplishments, Paul did. But he recognized how worthless his deeds were, and he knew that his religious zeal had actually blinded him to the plan and purpose of God. His persecution of the early church had put many believers in prison. Yet the Lord called this man to be His "chosen vessel" to take the gospel to the Gentiles. The grace of God had turned a murderer into a missionary.

A friend called on John Newton, author of the beloved hymn "Amazing Grace," in the later years of his life. A portion of Scripture was read, including the verse, "But by the grace of God I am what I am" (1 Corinthians 15:10). Newton then commented, "I am not what I ought to be. How imperfect and deficient! I am not what I wish to be. I abhor what is evil, and I would cleave to what is good. I am not what I hope to be. Soon I shall put off mortality, all sin, and imperfection. Yet though I am not what I ought to be, nor what I wish to be, nor what I hope to be, I can truly say I am not what I once was—a slave to sin and Satan. I can heartily join with the apostle and acknowledge, 'By the grace of God I am what I am.' "

If you have been saved through faith in Jesus' sacrifice on the cross, you can say that too. Thank God for His amazing grace!

—*Richard DeHaan*

Backstory

Among the influential Christians Newton befriended after he had become a Christian and given up slave trading were preachers George Whitfield and John Wesley and poet William Cowper.

♪ REFRAIN

A look at the life of John Newton should remind us that it is only by grace that any of us—sinners just like Newton—are redeemed by our Savior.

He Is Here!

From God's Hymnal: Psalm 145:13–21

The LORD is near to all who call upon Him. —Psalm 145:18

God's promise to be with His people (Psalm 145:18) is a wonderful gift that we sometimes take for granted. But there are times in every believer's life when His presence becomes a precious reality.

A few years ago I sank into an uncharacteristic period of anxiety and depression. After many years of spiritual and emotional stability, I was nearly overwhelmed with dark thoughts. I struggled to counteract the despair with the truths of God and the help of the Holy Spirit.

Then one night I went to a gospel concert. During the concert, I heard a song I was not familiar with. I listened as the group sang a song entitled, "He Is Here."

The song expressed one of the most familiar truths of the Bible—a truth I had long taken for granted—our God is with us. But how it spoke to me that night! It brought me unbelievable comfort, release, and hope. The Lord used that gospel song to spark a turnaround in my life. I began to appreciate God's presence in a fresh and invigorating way.

As God's children, we may think we should be exempt from emotional struggles. But we aren't.

If it seems as if God has left you, if you are despondent, if you feel alone and afraid, meditate on the truth of the song title "He Is Here."

—*David Egner*

Backstory

The song "He Is Here" was named the 1992 Dove Award Song of the Year, and it received a nomination for a Grammy Award.

REFRAIN

No matter what problem or concern has captured our attention, the simple fact that God is here with us should be our greatest weapon against that need.

The Love of God

From God's Hymnal: Ephesians 3:18–19

To know the love of Christ which passes knowledge. —Ephesians 3:19

The lyrics of the hymn "The Love of God" by Frederick Lehman (1868–1953) capture in word pictures the breathtaking magnitude of divine love:

Could we with ink the ocean fill
And were the skies of parchment made,
Were every stalk on earth a quill,
And every man a scribe by trade,
To write the love of God above
Would drain the ocean dry,
Nor could the scroll contain the whole
Though stretched from sky to sky.

Backstory

Frederick Lehman wrote this song in 1917 while working for a fruit-packing company in California putting oranges and lemons in crates. Some of the lyrics for the song were added later by using lines taken from a Jewish poem written in the eleventh century.

These marvelous lyrics echo Paul's response to the love of God. The apostle prayed that believers might "be able to comprehend with all the saints what is the width and length and depth and height—to know the love of Christ which passes knowledge" (Ephesians 3:18–19). In reflecting on these verses about God's love, some Bible scholars believe "width" refers to its worldwide embrace (John 3:16); "length," its existence through all ages (Ephesians 3:21); "depth," its profound wisdom (Romans 11:33); and "height," its victory over sin opening the way to heaven (Ephesians 4:8).

We are admonished to appreciate this amazing love. Yet as we expand our awareness of God's love, we soon realize that its full measure is beyond our understanding. Even if the ocean itself were filled with ink, using it to write about the love of God would drain it dry.

—*Dennis Fisher*

REFRAIN

Our weak efforts to describe the love of God lead to marvelous poetry—despite our inability to adequately explain it.

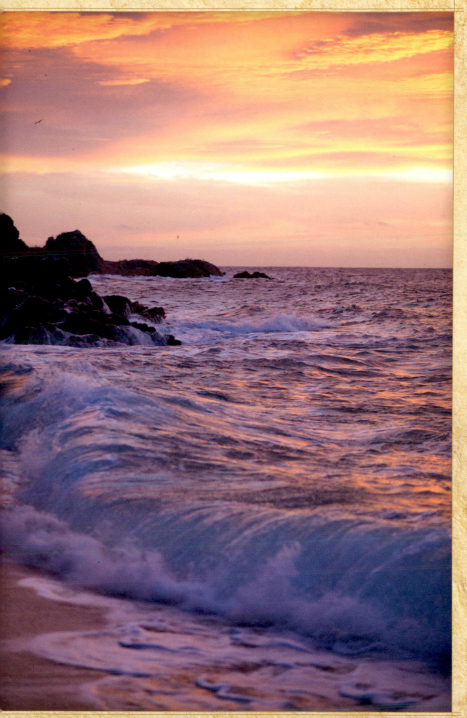

How Can We Keep from Singing?

From God's Hymnbook: Psalm 146

While I live I will praise the LORD; I will sing praises to my God while I have my being. —PSALM 146:2

Robert Lowry felt that preaching would be his greatest contribution in life. However, this nineteenth-century pastor (1826–1899) is best remembered for his gospel music and hymns. Lowry composed words or music for more than 500 songs, including "Christ Arose," "I Need Thee Every Hour," and "Shall We Gather at the River?"

In 1860, as the United States teetered on the brink of civil war, Lowry wrote these enduring words that focus not on threatening circumstances but on the unchanging Christ:

> *What though my joys and comforts die?*
> *The Lord my Savior liveth;*
> *What though the darkness gather round!*
> *Songs in the night He giveth:*
> *No storm can shake my inmost calm*
> *While to that refuge clinging;*
> *Since Christ is Lord of Heav'n and earth,*
> *How can I keep from singing?*

Lowry's confidence in God during difficult times echoes the psalmist's words: "Do not put your trust in princes, nor in a son of man, in whom there is no help. . . . Happy is he who has the God of Jacob for his help, whose hope is in the LORD his God" (Psalm 146:3–5).

Whether we react to life with faith or fear depends on our focus. Knowing that "the LORD shall reign forever" (v. 10), how can we keep from singing?

—*David McCasland*

🎵 REFRAIN

As we think of what circumstances might keep us from singing, we can remind ourselves that God is working in all of those situations to buoy our hearts.

Gaining from Losing

From God's Hymnal: Psalm 143

*Cause me to hear Your lovingkindness in the morning, for in You do I trust;
cause me to know the way in which I should walk, for I lift up my soul to You.*
—Psalm 143:8

The great composer Ludwig van Beethoven (1770–1827) lived much of his life in fear of deafness. He was concerned because he felt the sense of hearing was essential to creating music of lasting value.

When Beethoven discovered that the thing he feared most was coming rapidly upon him, he was almost frantic with anxiety. He consulted doctors and tried every possible remedy. But the deafness increased until at last all hearing was gone.

Beethoven finally found the strength he needed to go on despite his great loss. To everyone's amazement, he wrote some of his grandest music after he became totally deaf. With all distractions shut out, melodies flooded in on him as fast as his pen could write them down. His deafness became a great asset.

Many Christians can testify of the deeper joys experienced when a great loss isolated them from the world around them. It was then that they cried out to the Lord and could hear for the first time the voice of God reassuring them of His unfailing love and grace. It put a song of praise in their hearts.

Child of God, have you experienced a great loss? Don't lose hope. Call on the Lord. Trust Him and keep listening. If you do, you will gain even from loss.

—*Henry Bosch*

Backstory

Beethoven's marvelous music from his Ninth Symphony was used to accompany the words of Henry van Dyke's amazing poem "Joyful, Joyful, We Adore Thee." Beethoven's Ninth was written by the composer in the 1820s; van Dyke wrote the words in 1907.

REFRAIN

Amazingly, it is often in the darkest of moments that we see the light of God's love shining the brightest.

Are You Afraid?

From God's Hymnal: Psalm 56

Whenever I am afraid, I will trust in You. —Psalm 56:3

Hotly pursued by his enemies the Philistines, the psalmist David was understandably afraid. Who wouldn't be! In many circumstances fear is natural. God made us with that capacity. But this powerful emotion, unless controlled, can either stop us dead in our tracks or make us run like a scared rabbit.

David countered this paralysis/panic reaction by putting his faith in God and praising His Word. One Bible translation renders Psalm 56:4 this way: "In God, whose Word I praise, in God I trust; I will not be afraid."

Christians can find the same help today when gripped by fear of an enemy. Captain Dundy Aipoalani was an F-16 pilot during Operation Desert Storm. He wrote, "I was scared many times during my twenty-eight missions over Iraq and Kuwait, but I hung on to the cross of Jesus and trusted in His love. Sometimes on my missions I would get so nervous that I would sing, 'Jesus loves me, this I know, for the Bible tells me so.'" It was all he could remember, but it was enough to know that Jesus loved him. God said so.

Afraid? Trust God and remind yourself of His love for you in Christ. Fear may not suddenly evaporate, but trusting God and praising His Word will prevent panic and strengthen you to go on.

—*Dennis DeHaan*

Backstory

The popular little song "Jesus Loves Me, This I Know" was written in 1860 by a woman named Anna Bartlett Warner (she also wrote "We Would See Jesus"). The music was added a few years later by William Bradbury. An eclectic group of entertainers have recorded this song: Ray Stevens, Whitney Houston, Rosemary Clooney, the group Alabama, and Dionne Warwick.

 REFRAIN

Isn't it true that sometimes the simplest truths are the best truths when life confronts us with more than we think we can handle?

Worship His Majesty

From God's Hymnal: Revelation 19:11–16

And He has on His robe and on His thigh a name written: KING OF KINGS AND LORD OF LORDS. — REVELATION 19:16

Jack Hayford and his wife, Anna, were vacationing in Great Britain during the 25th anniversary of the coronation of Queen Elizabeth II in 1978. While there, the Hayfords saw constant reminders of royalty. That, along with visits to several castles, caused Hayford to sense what it might be like to be "raised as a child in such regal settings." With this in mind, he asked Anna to write down some lyrics one day as they drove through the countryside: Those words spoke of God's majesty, emphasizing the power and praise that goes to Jesus. Thus the glorious praise song "Majesty" was born.

In Scripture, Jesus is called "High Priest," "Prince of Peace," "Lamb of God," Bread of Life," "Light of the World," "Good Shepherd." But perhaps the most magnificent, awe-inspiring title is "King of Kings." It reminds us that His power far surpasses that of any mortal ruler. It suggests to us the splendor of the ultimate kingdom in which He will reign forever. What's most amazing is that we who know Christ as Savior are children of the King.

How should we respond? Hayford's song suggests that each day we should lift in praise Jesus' name as we give Him glory. Yes, our primary task in life is to worship His Majesty.

— *Dave Branon*

REFRAIN

What a difference it can make in our attitude and demeanor if we remember that we are children of the King!

"Bring Us Light"

From God's Hymnal: Luke 1:67–69

Through the tender mercy of our God, with which the Dayspring from on high has visited us; to give light to those who sit in darkness and the shadow of death, to guide our feet into the way of peace. —LUKE 1:78–79

As hard as she tried, Joni Eareckson could not get into the Christmas spirit. It was Christmas Eve, and she was seated in church with her friends. Candles lined the sanctuary. Boughs of green pine decked with red ribbon were everywhere. A soft snow swirled outside. Everything was perfect—except Joni.

As the congregation sang, she did not feel a single stirring of adoration or praise. "It's no use," her heart cried. "I'm a failure." So she sulked. Then the bittersweet, wistful strains of a familiar carol reached her heart. From "O Come, O Come, Immanuel" came the words, "And ransom captive Israel, that mourns in lonely exile here." This described her feelings exactly.

The song continued, "O come, Thou Dayspring, come and cheer our spirits by Thine advent here; O drive away the shades of night and pierce the clouds and bring us light!" "That's how I feel!" she cried out in her soul. She bowed and asked the Lord to take the gloom away and bring her cheer—and He did!

What happened to Joni happens to all who respond in faith to Jesus—whether they are receiving Him as their Savior or are renewing fellowship with Him. He came to drive away the darkness of guilt and gloom and replace it with the light of His joy and peace.

O come, Immanuel!

—*David Egner*

Backstory

Unlike most of the songs we sing today, "O Come, O Come, Immanuel" does not have a known author. The lyrics were apparently passed down through the centuries from the twelfth century and translated from Latin to English. The tune has been credited to songwriter Thomas Helmore in the mid-1800s.

REFRAIN

The promise that at any time we can call on our Immanuel, "God with us," for help can brighten our day and lighten our load.

Heaven without Jesus?

From God's Hymnal: Revelation 22:1–5

They shall see His face, and His name shall be on their foreheads.
—Revelation 22:4

When John W. Peterson (1921–2006) first started writing gospel melodies and lyrics, some were rejected by publishers. One such occurrence was especially disturbing to the young musician. Peterson had just written "Over the Sunset Mountains" after meditating on that glorious day when we will enter the joys of heaven and see the Savior. The music editor he approached seemed pleased with his song but made this small suggestion: "Take out the name Jesus, and enlarge a little more on heaven." Peterson thought, Heaven without Jesus? That is unthinkable! So he picked up his manuscript and left.

Soon another song came into his mind that expressed his heartfelt reaction:

> *I have no song to sing, but that of Christ my King;*
> *To Him my praise I'll bring forevermore!*
> *His love beyond degree, His death that ransomed me;*
> *Now and eternally, I'll sing it o'er.*

God honored John Peterson for not compromising the truth. Eventually both songs were published, and over the years they have brought comfort to many.

As a Christian, Peterson couldn't think of heaven without Christ. He knew that when believers are facing death, they are comforted in the knowledge that joy awaits them in the presence of their Lord.

My friend, are you looking forward to seeing Jesus in heaven?

—*Henry Bosch*

REFRAIN

Of all the benefits heaven promises, can there be any greater reality than the fact that we will be in the forever presence of our Savior?

Struggles and Songs

From God's Hymnal: Psalm 13

My heart shall rejoice in Your salvation. —PSALM 13:5

William Cowper (pronounced "Cooper"), an eighteenth-century English poet and hymn writer (1731–1800), struggled with recurring bouts of depression throughout his life. Perhaps that's why his hymns still touch us deeply during times when our life seems to be spinning out of control and we desperately want to trust God.

One of Cowper's best-known hymns, "God Moves in a Mysterious Way," contains these encouraging words:

> *Ye fearful saints, fresh courage take;*
> *The clouds ye so much dread*
> *Are big with mercy and shall break*
> *In blessings on your head.*

We often imagine that the triumphal songs of faith were penned by people who had already overcome their struggles. But the Bible's songbook—the Psalms—reminds us that the anguished cries of "How long, O LORD? Will You forget me forever? How long will You hide Your face from me?" sometimes occur in almost the same breath as "My heart shall rejoice in Your salvation. I will sing to the LORD, because He has dealt bountifully with me" (Psalm 13:1, 5–6).

In every struggle—mental, physical, emotional, or spiritual—our challenge is to move from the fear of being overwhelmed to the confidence that God has overcome. Cowper didn't find it easy, but he always found that God was greater than he had ever imagined.

Facing clouds today? Take courage! Your greatest praise to God may be sung in the darkest days of your life.

—*David McCasland*

Backstory

William Cowper was a close friend of John Newton, and they collaborated on a songbook called *Olney Hymns* published in 1779. Cowper also wrote "There Is a Fountain Filled with Blood."

♪ REFRAIN

Without the clouds, there can never be rain; without the rain, no growth. Don't dread the clouds; anticipate the gain.

Space Music

From God's Hymnal: Job 38:1–7

To what were [the earth's] foundations fastened? Or who laid its cornerstone, when the morning stars sang together, and all the sons of God shouted for joy?
—Job 38:6–7

One of NASA's observatories has discovered a giant black hole that hums. Located in the Perseus cluster of galaxies about 250 million light years from Earth, the black hole vibrates at the frequency of a B flat. But it is too low a pitch to be picked up by the human ear. Scientific instruments have placed the note at 57 octaves below middle C on a piano.

The idea of music and heavenly bodies is not new. In fact, when God revealed himself to Job, He asked: "Where were you when I laid the foundations of the earth? . . . When the morning stars sang together, and all the sons of God shouted for joy?" (Job 38:4, 7). At creation, songs of praise and shouts of joy resounded to God's glory.

A hymn by St. Francis of Assisi captures the awe and worship we feel when beholding the radiant sun by day or the star-studded sky at night.

> All creatures of our God and King,
> Lift up your voice and with us sing Alleluia, Alleluia!
> Thou burning sun with golden beam,
> Thou silver moon with softer gleam:
> O praise Him, O praise Him!

"The heavens declare the glory of God" (Psalm 19:1). Let's praise the One who made such beauty for us to enjoy!

—Dennis Fisher

Backstory

St. Francis lived from 1182 to 1226 in Italy, and this song was written near the end of his life. He apparently wrote more than fifty songs for the men who lived in the monastery where he served. Legend has it that Francis created the first manger scene to commemorate Christmas and Jesus' birth.

♫ REFRAIN

Looking for something to praise God about? Step outside at night and look into the sparkling sky and marvel that our creator God has flung millions of stars into place.

People Who Sing!

From God's Hymnal: Psalm 96

They sing the song of Moses, the servant of God, and the song of the Lamb, saying: "Great and marvelous are Your works, Lord God Almighty! Just and true are Your ways, O King of the saints!" —REVELATION 15:3

Emperor penguins love to sing. They are among the most musical creatures on earth. When courting, the male and female bow and sing to each other. Her voice is soft and gentle; he sings loud and long. After the mother penguin has laid her eggs, she goes off to the ocean for several weeks to feed. While she is gone, the father incubates the eggs and sings. After regaining her strength, the female comes back to the nest and sings as well. And shortly before a little one is hatched, if you lean your ear down close to the shell, you can hear the chick singing inside.

The people of God are also singers. When Moses led Israel out of Egypt, he paused to praise God in song (Exodus 15:1–18). Deborah sang in victory (Judges 5). David's songs were numerous. Many psalms begin with a reference to singing (66, 81, 89, 92, 95, 96, 98, 101, 138, 149). The disciples sang in the upper room (Mark 14:26). Paul instructed believers to sing (Ephesians 5:19; Colossians 3:16). And our verse for today tells of the song of the redeemed in heaven.

Are we singing Christians? Are we expressing the joy of the Lord in song? It may not always be on our lips, but it should resound in our hearts and minds. If you have no song, something is wrong. Christians are a people who can't help but sing!

—*David Egner*

Backstory

The biblical book of the Psalms is the part of the Bible that is most often set to music, which makes sense because some of the psalms were songs in the day in which they were penned (Songs of Ascent, for instance, in Psalms 120–134). There have been projects in which musicians have turned all 150 psalms into songs.

♪ REFRAIN

Being a singing Christian may be the best remedy for getting through those times that get a person down. Try being sorrowful while singing "How Great Is Our God."

Rest into It

From God's Hymnal: Romans 8:31–39

"Come to Me, all you who labor and are heavy laden, and I will give you rest."
—Matthew 11:28

The most enjoyable part of the stretch-and-flex exercise class I attend is the last five minutes. That's when we lie flat on our backs on our mats with the lights down low for relaxation. During one of those times, our instructor said softly, "Find a place where you can rest into." I thought of the best place to "rest into" mentioned in the words of a hymn by Cleland B. McAfee, "Near to the Heart of God."

Backstory

Cleland McAfee (1866–1944) pastored churches in Chicago and Brooklyn during his career. He also spent many years as a seminary professor.

There is a place of quiet rest,
Near to the heart of God,
A place where sin cannot molest,
Near to the heart of God.
O Jesus, blest Redeemer,
Sent from the heart of God,
Hold us who wait before Thee
Near to the heart of God.

This hymn was written in 1903 after the death of McAfee's two nieces from diphtheria. His church choir sang it outside the quarantined home of his brother, offering words of hope about God's heart of care.

The apostle Paul tells us that God has a heart of love for us (Romans 8:31–39). Nothing—not tribulation, distress, persecution, famine, nakedness, peril, sword, death, life, angels, principalities, powers, height, nor depth—is able to separate us from the enduring love of our God. "If God is for us, who can be against us?" (v. 31).

Whatever our stresses or concerns, the heart of God is the place to "rest into." Leave it all with Him, "for He cares for you" (1 Peter 5:7).

—*Anne Cetas*

 REFRAIN

The best way to rest from life's struggles is to lean on Jesus.

Mozart's Pet Bird

From God's Hymnal: Psalm 104:1–13

The birds of the heavens have their home; they sing among the branches.
—Psalm 104:12

Wolfgang Amadeus Mozart (1756–1791) is revered as a genius of musical composition. In one instance, he was even inspired by the melody of a bird. Mozart had a pet starling whose song so fascinated him that some say he wrote a piece of music based on the melody he heard in the bird's chirps.

Birds were also an inspiration to the psalmist. In Psalm 104, he praises God for caring for the living creatures He put on the earth. Included in his observations are birds who fly in the heavens above, perch in the branches of trees, and sing songs of heartfelt joy: "The birds of the heavens have their home; they sing among the branches" (v. 12). Nature filled the psalmist's heart with praise to God, and I think that must have included the musical sounds of the birds.

Often the marvels we see in creation prompt us to worship. This theme is repeated throughout Scripture: "The heavens declare the glory of God; and the firmament shows His handiwork" (Psalm 19:1). Creation's stimulus to praise need not be limited to the visual. It can also be widened to include hearing nature's songs. As we go about our daily routine, we can tune our hearts to the melodies God has placed in His creatures and let them serve as an added springboard of praise to the Creator.

Backstory

Mozart bought his pet starling on May 27, 1784, for thirty-four kreutzer (a German coin). The bird lived at the Mozart home until it died three years later. Like many of us have who have lost a pet, Mozart buried the deceased songbird in the backyard.

—*Dennis Fisher*

🎵 REFRAIN

Nature continually shouts God's praises through its beauty, magnificence, majesty, and resplendence. May we learn to be as effusive in our praise.

Meeting at the Fountain

From God's Hymnal: Revelation 7:9–17

The Lamb who is in the midst of the throne will shepherd them and lead them to living foundation of waters. —REVELATION 7:17

One of the outstanding composers of gospel hymns in the nineteenth century was Philip P. Bliss. Saved at an early age, he wrote such songs as "Hold the Fort," "Wonderful Words of Life," and "Almost Persuaded."

The story about the writing of one of his compositions is not too well known, but the song has blessed many. When Bliss joined evangelist D. L. Moody in Chicago, a great industrial exposition was being held. One of its central attractions was a grand fountain. It became the rallying point where people frequently gathered. One would say to another, "Will you meet me at the fountain?" The answer would be, "Yes, that's easy to find and a beautiful place to wait." Bliss was struck by those words, and it brought to his mind Revelation 7:17. This verse speaks of heaven and its fountains of living water and of the Lamb of God gathering there with His redeemed saints. This inspired Bliss to pen these words:

> Will you meet me at the fountain, when I reach the
>   glory land?
> There'll be music at the fountain; oh, be sure to meet
>   me there!

Nothing sinful or defiling can ever be allowed to enter that heavenly country. Only those who are cleansed by Jesus' blood can hope to enjoy the fellowship and blessing found there. The question posed by Philip Bliss in that gospel song is one we all must answer. Will you meet me there?

—*Henry Bosch*

Backstory

Philip Bliss became connected with D. L. Moody after attending a Moody revival and offering his services. Bliss worked with Moody for a time, but when Moody asked him to help with meetings in England, Bliss declined. Ira Sankey went instead, and he became synonymous with Moody.

♪ REFRAIN

Need something to praise God for today? Praise Him for the healing fountain of Jesus' love poured out for us on the cross. That's the meeting place for all sinners and their Savior.

Scriptural Songs

From God's Hymnal: Colossians 3:15–17

Let the word of Christ dwell in you richly . . . in psalms and hymns and spiritual songs, singing with grace in your hearts to the Lord. —COLOSSIANS 3:16

The beloved songwriter John W. Peterson was a master at using Scripture in his songs. When I was a teenager in the church choir, we performed his cantata "Jesus Is Coming" and sang these words taken from 2 Timothy 3:1–2: "In the last days perilous times shall come: for men shall be lovers of themselves." Then he wrote of the grim signs that we would recognize in the last days (vv. 2–7). The steady cadence of his music helps me remember that list even today.

While some of us have trouble memorizing verses from God's Word, something in our brain helps us to remember words in songs. If we analyze some of our favorite Christian songs and choruses, we find that they have been derived from Scripture. Thus, we can use the memory boost of music to hide away God-breathed words in our hearts (2 Timothy 3:16). Songs such as "Open the Eyes of My Heart" (Isaiah 6:9–10; Ephesians 1:18) or favorites like "Thy Word Have I Hid in My Heart" (Psalm 119:11, 105) are taken from the Bible. With these words hidden in our memory, a song of praise comes quickly to our lips.

No matter what kind of voice you have, when you sing the words of Scripture back to God, it is sweet music to His ears.

—*Cindy Hess Kasper*

Backstory

Songwriter Paul Baloche didn't "write" the song "Open the Eyes of My Heart" as much as he "sang" it. As he was leading singing one day at his church and thinking of Ephesians 1:18, he simply began strumming his guitar and singing, "Open the eyes of my heart, Lord." On his blog he said that the song, "pretty much rolled off my tongue."

♪ REFRAIN

As we think about allowing God to open the eyes of our hearts, let's contemplate what kinds of things He wants us to see.

Bird Song

From God's Hymnal: Psalm 104:24–35

Break forth in song, rejoice, and sing praises. —Psalm 98:4

Why do birds sing? Birds sing "because they can and because they must," says David Rothenberg, a professor at the New Jersey Institute of Technology. "Songs are used to attract mates and defend territories, but the form is much more than function. Nature is full of beauty, and of music."

Backstory

John Donne (1572–1631), who lived most of his life in England and who was educated at Oxford University, penned such famous lines as "never send to know for whom the bell tolls; it tolls for thee," "no man is an island," and "death be not proud" in his many poems and sermons and devotional works.

Birds sing because they have a syrinx instead of a larynx. The syrinx is the bird's voice box, an organ that lies deep in a bird's chest and is uniquely fashioned for song. That, at least, is the natural explanation for their gift.

But I ask again, why do birds sing? Because their Creator put a song in their hearts. Each bird is "heaven's high and holy muse," said John Donne, created to draw our hearts up to our Creator. They are reminders that He has given us a song that we may sing His praise.

So when you hear God's little hymn-birds singing their hearts out, remember to sing your own song of salvation. Lift up your voice— harmonious, hoarse, or harsh—and join with them in praise to our Creator, Redeemer, and Lord.

The birds of the air "sing among the branches," Israel's poet observes. "[Therefore] I will sing to the LORD as long as I live; I will sing praise to my God while I have my being" (Psalm 104:12, 33).

—*David Roper*

REFRAIN

Birds. Faith. Beauty. Love. Family. Jesus. Nature. Jobs. Health. The list can go on and on as we contemplate what we have to sing about. Have you sung to God today?

The Music of Joy

From God's Hymnal: Nehemiah 12:27–43

God had made them rejoice with great joy . . . , so that the joy of Jerusalem was heard afar off. —NEHEMIAH 12:43

Several years ago, during a Christian men's conference in Boulder, Colorado, I stood with 50,000 men as we sang "All Hail the Power of Jesus' Name." The volume of the singing was incredible in the football stadium, and I've often wondered how it sounded outside. Could people hear it as they walked through a nearby park, sat on their patios, or drove by in cars? What impression did it leave with them?

That great sound of praise reminded me of what is described in today's Bible reading. The book of Nehemiah begins with a confession, continues with a construction project, and ends with a concert. The entire story is a study in God's faithfulness and power.

After years of hard work despite opposition, the wall of Jerusalem was rebuilt. At the dedication, two "thanksgiving choirs" stood on the wall to praise God. We are told that "the singers sang loudly . . . . God had made them rejoice with great joy . . . , so that the joy of Jerusalem was heard afar off" (Nehemiah 12:42–43).

Joy cannot be contained. It must break out in praise to God through songs of thanksgiving. Whether those who hear our outpouring of joy understand it or not, it will resound as a chorus that cannot be ignored—the music of lives lived out in praise to God.

—*David McCasland*

Backstory

The song "All Hail the Power of Jesus' Name" was first released to the public in 1779 in a magazine that was edited by Augustus Toplady, the man who wrote "Rock of Ages." The author of "All Hail . . . " was Edward Perronet (1726–1792), a friend of John and Charles Wesley.

 REFRAIN

While it is God to whom our praise songs are sung, there are times when others who overhear our music of adoration are also drawn heavenward.

His Way

From God's Hymnal: Matthew 26:36–46

O My Father, if it is possible, let this cup pass from Me; nevertheless, not as I will, but as you will. —MATTHEW 26:39

A question about the title of a hymn took me back to a wonderful old song I grew up singing in church called "Let Him Have His Way with Thee." The chorus says:

> *His power can make you what you ought to be,*
> *His blood can cleanse your heart and make you free,*
> *His love can fill your soul, and you will see*
> *'Twas best for Him to have His way with thee.*

Even when we know that God's way is best for us, we may still struggle to obey Him. When Christ our Savior faced the horrible reality of bearing our sins on the cross, He agonized in prayer, saying, "O My Father, if it is possible, let this cup pass from Me; nevertheless, not as I will, but as You will" (Matthew 26:39). Jesus, who lived to do His Father's will, struggled and prayed, then willingly obeyed. And He can help us as we grapple with the difficult choices in our lives.

C. S. Lewis wrote: "There are only two kinds of people in the end: those who say to God, 'Thy will be done,' and those to whom God says, in the end, 'Thy will be done.'" If we continually choose our own way, He will eventually allow us to suffer the consequences.

It's best to surrender to God now. If we do, we'll have the assurance that His way is best for us.

—*David McCasland*

Backstory

The man who wrote "Let Him Have His Way with Thee," Cyrus Nusbaum (1861–1937), was an ordained pastor. During World War I, he was a US Army captain who served in France.

♪ REFRAIN

Submitting to God's will now will save us the trouble of admitting our faults and seeking forgiveness for disobedience later.

"Yes, We'll Gather at the River"

From God's Hymnal: Revelation 22:1–5

And he showed me a pure river of water of life, clear as crystal, proceeding from the throne of God and of the Lamb. —REVELATION 22:1

Many heart-stirring songs have been written by gifted Christian poets and composers who were inspired by real-life experiences. Pastor Robert Lowry (1826–1899), for example, penned the words and music of a hymn during an epidemic that was raging in the city of Philadelphia.

Backstory

A portion of this song was used in a movie called *The Trip to Bountiful*, a 1985 film in which Geraldine Page won an Academy Award. It was also sung at the memorial service of US Supreme Court Justice William O. Douglas in 1980.

On a sultry afternoon in July, he sat in his study thinking about the many friends and loved ones who had recently been claimed by death. As he pondered the situation, he asked himself: Why do hymn writers say so much about the mournful river of death we must cross but so little about the delightful river of life that Christians will enjoy in the new heaven and earth? Moved by that thought, he wrote the verses that were to immortalize his name long after his excellent sermons were forgotten.

Because it brought comfort to thousands and continues to console grieving hearts everywhere, "Shall We Gather at the River?" remains a favorite today, more than 150 years after it was written. The first verse asks,

> Shall we gather at the river, where bright angel feet have trod,
> With its crystal tide forever flowing by the throne of God?

Friend, when eternity dawns, will you be a member of the joyous company of the redeemed who will gather to praise the Lord at that crystal stream?

—*Henry Bosch*

REFRAIN

Imagine arriving in heaven and seeing for the first time both the saints of earth and the author of our salvation—at the "beautiful river."

Only from Above

From God's Hymnal: Psalm 104:21–28

Every good gift and every perfect gift is from above, and comes down from the Father of lights, with whom there is no variation or shadow of turning.
—JAMES 1:17

The sustaining and providing hand of our loving heavenly Father is always outstretched toward us. Yet we are often prone to forget the source of all the good that comes into our lives.

In 1808, just a year before the death of Franz Joseph Haydn, a grand performance of his outstanding oratorio *The Creation* took place in Vienna. The composer himself, though old and feeble, was there for the occasion. As the orchestra and chorus burst forth with full power into the passage, "And there was light," a crescendo of applause broke out. Moved by this response, the elderly musician struggled to his feet. Summoning all his strength, he raised his trembling arms upward, crying, "No, no! Not from me, but from thence—from heaven above comes all!" The old master had made his point in a dramatic and unforgettable manner.

The bountiful provisions for our physical needs and the amazing grace that makes us joint heirs with Christ all come from God. Let us acknowledge our dependence upon Him and humbly say, "When I consider Your heavens, the work of Your fingers, the moon and the stars, which You have ordained, what is man that You are mindful of him?" (Psalm 8:3–4). Surely "every good gift and every perfect gift is from above."

—*Paul Van Gorder*

Backstory

According to biographer Dave Massey, Franz Joseph Haydn (1732–1809) was so taken with doing justice to the creation in the work of the same name that, in Haydn's words, "Every day I fell to my knees and prayed to God to grant me the strength" to finish it. He was sixty-six years old when he finished the oratorio.

♪ REFRAIN

Humility in our lives stems from the realization that all glory and honor belong to God for the good gifts He has given us.

Now Is the Time

From God's Hymnal: Luke 2:8–20

Glory to God in the highest! —LUKE 2:14

During our church's Christmas celebration, I watched the choir members assemble in front of the congregation while the music director rifled through papers on a slim black stand. The instruments began, and the singers launched into the well-known song "Come, Now Is the Time to Worship."

Although I expected to hear a time-honored Christmas carol, I smiled at the appropriate choice of music. Earlier that week I had been reading Luke's account of Jesus' birth, and I noticed that the first Christmas lacked our modern-day parties, gifts, and feasting—but it did include worship.

After the angel announced Jesus' birth to some wide-eyed shepherds, a chorus of angels began "praising God and saying: 'Glory to God in the highest!' " (Luke 2:13–14). The shepherds responded by running to Bethlehem where they found the newborn King lying in a barnyard bassinet. They returned to their fields "glorifying and praising God for all the things that they had heard and seen" (v. 20). Coming face to face with the Son inspired the shepherds to worship the Father.

Today, consider your response to Jesus' arrival on earth. Is there room for worship in your heart to celebrate His birth?

—*Jennifer Benson Schuldt*

Backstory

One day during a wilderness time in his life, Brian Doerksen took an early morning walk. As he strolled through his London neighborhood, the idea and the melody for this song began to come to him. He sang this first part of the song over and over until he arrived at home and could put the music and words down on paper.

♪ REFRAIN

As we celebrate the baby's birth, why shouldn't worship be our first response? After all, this was our Creator, our Savior, and our Lord lying in that manger!

Public Praise

From God's Hymnal: Psalm 96

Declare His glory among the nations, His wonders among all peoples.
—Psalm 96:3

I love the YouTube video of people in a food court of a mall, who in the midst of their ordinary lives were suddenly interrupted by someone who stood up and boldly began singing the "Hallelujah Chorus." To the surprise of everyone, another person got up and joined the chorus, and then another, and another. Soon the food court was resounding with the celebrative harmonies of Handel's masterpiece. A local opera company had planted their singers in strategic places so that they could joyfully interject the glory of God into the everyday lives of lunching shoppers.

Every time I watch that video, it moves me to tears. It reminds me that bringing the glory of God into the ordinary situations of our world through the beautiful harmonies of Christlikeness is exactly what we are called to do. Think of intentionally interjecting God's grace into a situation where some undeserving soul needs a second chance; of sharing the love of Christ with someone who is needy; of being the hands of Jesus that lift up a weary friend; or of bringing peace to a confusing and chaotic situation.

As the psalmist reminds us, we have the high and holy privilege of declaring "His glory among the nations, His wonders among all peoples" (Psalm 96:3).

—*Joe Stowell*

Backstory

As the food court rendition moved along, patrons began to join in, to stand, to take photos with their phones—and when the song was over, they erupted in applause. Many were in tears as God's praise rang throughout that section of the mall.

REFRAIN

What a joy to see the radiance on people's faces as they stop whatever they are doing and extend joyous praise to our heavenly Father.

Change of Plans

From God's Hymnal: Proverbs 16:1–9

A man's heart plans his way, but the LORD *directs his steps.* —PROVERBS 16:9

It was Christmas Eve in Oberndorf, Austria, in 1818. Joseph Mohr, the vicar of the church, had written a new song for the Christmas Eve service and the organist Franz Gruber had set it to music. But the organ in the village church broke down. So Gruber grabbed a guitar and accompanied Mohr in the first-ever rendition of "Silent Night."

The story doesn't end there, however. When a man came to fix the organ, Gruber tested it by playing the new song. The repairman liked the song so much that he took a copy of it back to his own village. There, four daughters of a village glovemaker learned the song and began singing it in concerts all over the region. Because of that faulty organ, this new Christmas song blessed people all over Austria—and eventually the world.

When things break or when plans change, how should we respond? Often we fret and worry because we don't have the control we would like to have. That's when we need to step back, trust God, and wait to see how He will use the situation for His glory. The changes in our lives may not give the world something as remarkable as "Silent Night," but because God is in charge we can be sure that "all is calm, all is bright."

—*Dave Branon*

Backstory

Only one other song written by Joseph Mohr (1792–1848) and Franz Gruber has been discovered. It is called "Te Deum," and it was not found until 2006 among the archives of a parish where Mohr once served.

REFRAIN

Because of Jesus' miraculous appearance on earth and the "dawn of redeeming grace," we can sing "Alleluia" to our King. Christ the Savior is born!

All Is Well

From God's Hymnal: Psalm 46:1–3

Let your conduct be without covetousness; be content with such things as you have. For He Himself has said, "I will never leave you nor forsake you." —HEBREWS 13:5

Recently, my husband and I were reacquainted with a young man we had known as a child many years ago. We fondly reminisced about a Christmas program when Matthew had sung—in a perfect boy soprano—the song "All Is Well" by Wayne Kirkpatrick and Michael W. Smith. It was a wonderful memory of a song beautifully sung. It is a song that speaks of the birth of Emmanuel—our Savior and our Lord, and it reminds us of those glorious words in the song's title.

To hear the words "all is well" at Christmastime is comforting to many. But some people are unable to absorb the message because their lives are in turmoil. They've experienced the loss of a loved one, persistent unemployment, a serious illness, or depression that will not go away. Their hearts loudly cry out, "All is not well—not for me!"

But for those of us who celebrate the birth of our Savior—despite the dark night of the soul we may experience—all is well because of Christ. We are not alone in our pain. God is beside us and promises never to leave (Hebrews 13:5). He promises that His grace will be sufficient (2 Corinthians 12:9). He promises to supply all our needs (Philippians 4:19). And He promises us the amazing gift of eternal life (John 10:27–28).

As we review God's promises, we can agree with the poet John Greenleaf Whittier, who wrote, "Before me, even as behind, God is, and all is well."

—*Cindy Hess Kasper*

Backstory

According to an article by Thom Granger, Michael W. Smith wrote the music for the song "All Is Well" before he had the words. After he developed the tune, he asked a few people to pen the lyrics. Grammy Award–winning composer Wayne Kirkpatrick finally came up with the words.

♪ REFRAIN

The face of trouble looks like pain, desertion, mistreatment, and sadness. The face of hope looks like Jesus, our Lord and Savior who makes all things well.

Happiness and Faith

From God's Hymnal: Romans 8:28–39

Now may the God of hope fill you with all joy and peace in believing, that you may abound in hope by the power of the Holy Spirit. — ROMANS 15:13

The chorus of the old hymn "At the Cross" concludes with these cheerful words: "And now I am happy all the day!" I don't know about you, but I can't honestly say that just because I know Jesus as my Savior I'm happy all day. I'm a rather optimistic person and I don't let much get me down, but some circumstances don't warm my heart and make me smile.

Troubles may make us wonder: Isn't our faith supposed to make us happy all the time? Shouldn't Jesus shelter us from harm and danger?

Some people teach these things, but the Bible doesn't. God's Word makes it clear that we will have trouble. In Romans 8, for example, the apostle Paul talked frankly about tough times we could face (vv. 35–39). The fact is, Jesus doesn't protect us from all trouble, but His love and His companionship guide us as we go through it.

A more realistic attitude than being "happy all the day" is one stated by a Christian who said, "Now that I'm saved, I'm happier when I am down than I was when I was happy before I was saved."

With Jesus Christ, we can have real joy and make it through even the bad times.

—Dave Branon

Backstory

Fanny Crosby, who penned so many of the timeless classics in our hymnbooks, was greatly influenced by the song "At the Cross," which was penned by Isaac Watts. Apparently she was attending revival meetings at a crisis time in her life, and the words "Here, Lord, I give my self away 'tis all that I can do" enlightened her soul.

REFRAIN

The true worth of our salvation is not superficial happiness but deep and lasting peace—a peace for which we have no adequate words.

More Than a Conqueror

From God's Hymnal: 2 Corinthians 12:1–10

We are more than conquerors through Him who loved us. —Romans 8:37

Fanny Crosby, composer of thousands of songs, was truly "more than a conqueror." When she was only six weeks old, faulty treatment of an eye infection resulted in lifelong blindness. By age eight, having fought and won over discouragement, she wrote this poem:

Oh, what a happy soul am I, although I cannot see!
I am resolved that in this world contented I shall be.
How many blessings I enjoy that other people don't.
To weep and sigh because I'm blind, I cannot—and I won't!

Instead of weeping and sighing, Fanny Crosby dedicated her blindness to God. Out of her rich Christian experience she composed numerous gospel hymns. In her testimonial song "Blessed Assurance," she seemed to forget that she was blind. Phrases like "Visions of rapture now burst on my sight" or "Watching and waiting, looking above" expressed what she called "a foretaste of glory divine."

Do you long to know and apply her secret? Consider this: While many of us seek Christ for what we can get, Fanny Crosby sought Christ for what she could become through Him—more than a conqueror (Romans 8:37). Even through times of extreme distress, God's grace is sufficient (2 Corinthians 12:9), and He works to make us more like His Son. We all need to ask ourselves: Is our Christian life about getting or becoming?

—*Joanie Yoder*

Backstory

Mistreated by a charlatan posing as a doctor, Fanny Crosby became blind at two months. Shortly after that, her father died. Struggling to survive, her mother became a maid. A grandmother was forced to raise her. Fanny's faith and her determination enabled her to write this poem at age eight and address Congress at age twenty-three.

♪ REFRAIN

Instead of allowing our circumstances to drag us down, it is better to allow our faith and our Savior to lift us up to unknown heights with His sufficient grace.

The Doctor's Bible

From God's Hymnal: Acts 26:9–18

Therefore, if anyone is in Christ, he is a new creation; old things have passed away; behold, all things have become new. —2 CORINTHIANS 5:17

A great transformation takes place in the sinner's heart when he is convicted by the Spirit of God.

Take the case of William Mackay (1839–1885). He had been brought up by a godly, praying mother, who gave him a Bible with his name inscribed inside the front cover when he went off to medical school. During his training, he renounced his mother's faith and began to drink heavily. He even pawned his Bible so he could buy more liquor.

Eventually, he became a medical doctor. One day as he tended an accident victim, the injured person asked Dr. Mackay if he would send for the man's landlady. He wanted her to bring "the book."

The patient never recovered, and after he died, Dr. Mackay was curious about "the book." A nurse helped him find the book—a Bible.

When the doctor opened the Bible, he saw his name written inside. This was the same book he had pawned years earlier to fuel his thirst for alcohol. Remembering his mother's love, under deep conviction of sin, and recalling John 3:16, he trusted Jesus as His Savior.

Not long afterward, Mackay penned the lyrics of the gospel song "Revive Us Again." The opening words were part of his new witness for Christ: "We praise Thee, O God, for the Son of Thy love, for Jesus who died and is now gone above."

Friend, the Lord Jesus can transform you as He did William Mackay and use you for His glory.

—*Henry Bosch*

Backstory

Cliff Barrows, a longtime part of Billy Graham's crusades, likes to tell about the time in Australia when two large groups of people, separated by two city blocks, sang parts of "Revive Us Again" antiphonally. One group of 80,000 sang "Hallelujah," and the other group of a similar size sang "Thine the glory."

♪ REFRAIN

The hard work of redemption is done. All that's left for even the worst sinner is to accept Jesus' free gift of salvation.

Scripture Index

OUR DAILY BREAD WRITERS

Henry Bosch
The first editor of *Our Daily Bread*, Henry loved to sing—and actually did some recording for Radio Bible Class in its early years.

Dave Branon
An editor with Discovery House Publishers, Dave has been involved with *Our Daily Bread* since the 1980s. He has written several books, including *Beyond the Valley* and *Stand Firm*, both DHP publications.

Anne Cetas
After becoming a Christian in her late teens, Anne was introduced to *Our Daily Bread* right away and began reading it. Now she reads it for a living as the managing editor of *Our Daily Bread*.

Bill Crowder
A former pastor who is now an associate teacher for RBC Ministries, Bill travels extensively as a Bible conference teacher, sharing God's truths with fellow believers in Malaysia and Singapore and other places where RBC has international offices.

Dennis DeHaan
When Henry Bosch retired, Dennis became the second managing editor of *Our Daily Bread*. A former pastor, he loved preaching and teaching the Word of God.

Richard DeHaan
Son of the founder of RBC Ministries, Dr. M. R. DeHaan, Richard was responsible for the ministry's entrance into television. Under his leadership, *Day of Discovery*, the ministry's long-running TV program, made its debut in 1968.

David Egner
A retired RBC editor and longtime *Our Daily Bread* writer, David was also a college professor during his working career. In fact, he was a writing instructor for both Anne Cetas and Julie Ackerman Link at Cornerstone University.

Dennis Fisher

As a research editor at RBC Ministries, Dennis uses his theological training to guarantee biblical accuracy. He is also an expert in C. S. Lewis studies.

Vernon Grounds

A longtime college president (Denver Seminary) and board member for RBC Ministries, Vernon's life story was told in the Discovery House Publishers book *Transformed by Love*.

Cindy Hess Kasper

An editor for the RBC publication *Our Daily Journey*, Cindy began writing for *Our Daily Bread* in 2006.

Julie Ackerman Link

A book editor by profession, Julie has written for *Our Daily Bread* since 2000. Her book *Above All, Love* was published in 2008 by Discovery House Publishers.

David McCasland

Living in Colorado, David enjoys the beauty and grandeur of God's creation as displayed in the Rocky Mountains. An accomplished biographer, David has written several books, including *Oswald Chambers: Abandoned to God* and *Eric Liddell: Pure Gold*.

Haddon Robinson

Haddon has taught hundreds of young preachers the art of preaching. He is former president of Denver Seminary and served for many years as a professor at Gordon-Conwell Theological Seminary.

David Roper

David Roper lives in Idaho, where he takes advantage of the natural beauty of his state. He has been writing for *Our Daily Bread* since 2000, and he has published several successful books with Discovery House Publishers.

Our Daily Bread Writers

Jennifer Benson Schuldt

Chicagoan Jennifer Schuldt writes from the perspective of a mom of a growing family. She has written for *Our Daily Bread* since 2010, and she also pens articles for another RBC publication: *Our Daily Journey*.

Joe Stowell

As president of Cornerstone University, Joe stays connected to today's young adults in a leadership role. A popular speaker and a former pastor, Joe has written a number of books over the years, including *Strength for the Journey* and *Jesus Nation*.

Herb Vander Lugt

For many years, Herb was the research editor at RBC Ministries, responsible for checking the biblical accuracy of the booklets published by RBC. A World War II veteran, Herb spent several years as a pastor before his RBC tenure began.

Paul Van Gorder

A writer for *Our Daily Bread* in the 1980s and 1990s, Paul was a noted pastor and Bible teacher—both in the Atlanta area where he lived and through the *Day of Discovery* TV program.

Joanie Yoder

Joanie and her husband established a Christian rehabilitation center for drug addicts in England many years ago. Widowed in 1982, she wrote with hope about true dependence on God and His life-changing power. Joanie was the author of the book *Finding the God-Dependent Life*.

NOTES

NOTES

Note to the Reader

The publisher invites you to share your response to the message of this book by writing Discovery House Publishers, P.O. Box 3566, Grand Rapids, MI 49501, U.S.A. For information about other Discovery House books, music, or DVDs, contact us at the same address or call 1-800-653-8333. Find us on the Internet at dhp.org or send an e-mail to books@dhp.org.